FUGITIVE COLOURS

Other titles by Liz Lochhead

POETRY

Memo for Spring (Reprographia, 1972)
Islands (Print Studio Press, 1978)
The Grimm Sisters (Next Editions, 1981)
Dreaming Frankenstein (Polygon, 1984)
True Confessions and New Clichés (Polygon, 1985)
Bagpipe Muzak (Penguin, 1991)
The Colour of Black & White (Polygon, 2003)
A Choosing (Polygon, 2011)

PLAYS

Blood and Ice (Methuen, 1984)
Mary Queen of Scots Gets Her Head Chopped Off (Penguin, 1988)
Dracula (Penguin, 1988)
Tartuffe (Nick Hern, 1998)
Perfect Days (Nick Hern, 1999)
Medea (Nick Hern, 2000)
Miseryguts (Nick Hern, 2002)
Thebans (Nick Hern, 2003)
Good Things (Nick Hern, 2006)
Educating Agnes (Nick Hern, 2008)
Five Plays (Nick Hern, 2012)

Fugitive Colours

LIZ LOCHHEAD

First published in Great Britain in 2016 by
Polygon, an imprint of Birlinn Ltd
West Newington House, 10 Newington Road
Edinburgh, EH9 1QS

www.polygonbooks.co.uk

ISBN: 978-1-84697-345-1

4

The publishers acknowledge investment from Creative Scotland
towards the publication of this book.

British Library Cataloguing-in-Publication Data
A catalogue record for this book is available on request
from the British Library.

Typeset in Verdigris MVB by 3btype.com
Printed and bound by TJ International, Padstow, Cornwall

for Tom, always

Contents

Love and Grief, Elegies and Promises

The Light Comes Back

Ekphrasis, Etcetera

Kidspoems and Bairnsangs

Makar Songs, Occassional and Performance Pieces Mainly

Love and Grief,
Elegies and Promises

Favourite Place

We would be snaking up Loch Lomond, the
road narrow and winding after the turn at Tarbet,
and we'd be bending branches as we slid
through the green and dripping overhang of the trees.
All the bickering over the packing, and the – as usual –
much, much later-than-we'd-meant-to leaving,
all that falling from us,
our moods lifting, lightening, becoming *our good mood*
the more miles we put
between our freed and weekend selves and Glasgow.

Driving in the dark meant: slot in another CD
without even looking at what it was,
another any-old silver-disc from the zippered case
that, when you reminded me, I'd have quickly stuffed
far too full and randomly, then jammed it,
last minute, into the top of my rucksack.
Golden oldies, yours or mine, whose favourite?
Anyway, the music would spool us through Tyndrum,
past the shut Real Food Café where other days we like to stop,
and over moonscape Rannoch Moor to the
moonlit majesty of Glencoe,
over the bridge at Ballachulish, past Corran
with the ferry stilled and the loch like glass;
we'd be wriggling along Loch Linnhe then straighten up
past the long strip of darkened lochside big hotels and their
Vacancies or *No Vacancies* signs
to 30 mph Fort William –
Full-Of-Rain-Town-With-Its-Limitless-Litres-In-A-Mist! –
we'd shout it out and we'd be honouring a
long-ago and someone else's
family pass-the-time
car-journey game we never even played, but Michael,
proud of his teenage wordsmith son,
once told us about – and it has stuck.

We'd be speeding up now, taking the bend's wide sweep as
we bypass the sleeping town, making for
the second-last turn-off: *Mallaig and The Road To the Isles.*
And you'd say,
'Last thirty miles, Lizzie, we'll be there by midnight'.

The always longest fifteen miles from Glenfinnan to Lochailort
and a wee cheer at the last turn,
down past the big house and the fish farm,
beyond the lay-by – full of travellers' ramshackle vans
now the yellow's on the broom again –
our eyes peeled now for the white-painted stone so we'll not miss
the overgrown entrance to the field of caravans.

There would be that sigh of
always-glad-to-see our old van still standing,
opening the door, the sniffing – no dampness, no mice . . .
I'd be unloading the first cool-bags of food,
while you'd be round the van's side, down in the mud
turning the stopcock for the water,
fixing the gas – and soon,
breathing a big sigh, laughing in relief at
how that huge stag that had suddenly filled the windscreen a mile
    back
stopping our hearts as – ho! – we'd shouted our alarm –
had somehow astonishly leapt free, was gone,
and no harm done,
we'd be lighting candles, pouring a dram,
drinking the first cup of tea
from the old black and white teapot.

And tonight the sky would be huge with stars.
Tomorrow there would be the distant islands
cut out of sugar paper, or else cloud, the rain in great veils
coming in across the water, the earliest tenderest
feathering of green on the trees, mibbe autumn
laying bare the birches stark white.
There would be blood-red rowan berries, that bold robin

eating from my plate again, or – for a week or two in May –
the elusive, insistent cuckoo,
or else the slow untidy flapping of the flight of the heron,
the oil-black cormorant's disappear-and-dive,
shifts of sun, double or even treble rainbows.
The waterfall would be a wide white plume or a
thin silver trickle, depending . . .
There would be bracken's early unfurling or
late summer's heather pinking and purpling over, there'd be
a plague of hairy caterpillars and the last drunken bees.
Mibbe you'd nudge me, and, hushed,
again we'd watch that otter swim to shore
on New Year's Day with a big fish in its mouth, emerge
so near us on the flat rocks we
wouldn't dare to breathe as we'd watch it,
unconcerned, oblivious,
make a meal of eating it before our eyes.
Or it would be a late Easter this year and,
everywhere along the roadside,
the chrome-yellow straight-out-of-the-tube-and-
laid-on-with-a palette-knife brashness, the
amazing coconut smell of the gorse.

But tonight you are three months dead
and I must pull down the bed and lie in it alone.
Tomorrow, and every day in this place
these words of Sorley MacLean's will echo through me:
The world is still beautiful, though you are not in it.
And this will not be a consolation
but a further desolation.

Persimmons

for Tom

You must've
loved
those three globes of gorgeous orange
dense and glowing in our winter kitchen
enough
to put coloured pencil and biro to the
reddest page left in your rainbow sketchbook
and make this drawing of
three persimmons in that Chinese bowl.

The supermarket flagged them up as
this season's sharon fruit
but we prefer *persimmon* (for
didn't it seem the rose of
their other name
would neither taste or sound as sweet,
would be a fruit of quite
another colour?)

Such strange fruit . . . we bit and ate,
enjoyed.
Before we did you drew them.
– *oh*, you'd say, *so what?*
(drawing, to you, is as everyday as apples)
but I know
they'd have come and gone like Christmas
if you'd not put them down
and made them worth more than the paper
they're inscribed on – see
those deft soft strokes of
aquamarine and white that
make our table-top lie flat, the fruits
plump out real and round and

perfectly persimmon-coloured
upon their lilac shadows in the bowl's deep –
still life
still life, sweetheart,
in what's already eaten and done with.

Now, looking, I can taste again.

A Handselling, 2006

I Twenty-One-Year-Old

On our first night at Jura Lodge you say,
'here's a bottle of the Twenty-One-Year-Old,
hey Lizzie, let's taste . . . ' and we toast
– once we've managed to track two nip glasses down –
'*oh there they are of course, my deah,*
on the decanter tray,
mayhap, in the Music Room!'
I laugh, oh I have to, as you slosh us each
a generous inch or more of gold, yes
you gently clink your glass with mine
and we toast our good fortune and the holiday to come.

All holidays
are whole small lives lived somewhere else
and all lives consist, in part, of habits
but we don't yet know this will be
one of the habits of this holiday –
on the long
light
nights of July
to sit astride that pair of purple velvet stools in the big
bay window of the Music Room looking out to the bay
with our
big brand-new sketch books balanced before us and
something more than twenty-one-years-old and easy-listening
playing – like old Van Morrison
predicting *it's a marvellous night for a moondance*
or Dylan groaning out *tangled up in blue*
as I scrabble for that and every other colour, for
on the little gaming table between us
a jumble of oil pastels and coloured conté crayon
is rolling around our rested whisky glasses –
occasionally savoured and sipped from, but never refilled –

as busily, fluently, more or less silently,
we sketch and scratch away and scribble
not stopping till – late – all the last of the light is gone
and we can't see
either what we're drawing or the marks we've made.

It'll be tomorrow
before I can enjoy the garish glad-handed sweep
you've made of a bit of the bay and pier and shrug
to see how hopeless was my
daft task of putting down the ever-changing sky
with its bands and streaks and shifting clouds
and almost every colour
except
sky blue.
But in spite of what
– on paper – neither of us captured
neither of us I'd bet
has ever been happier or easier with a crayon in our hands
since we were five years old –
nor less self-critical about the outcome, so
we can look at the nothing much we've caught
(*happiness writes white* said Philip Larkin) and
remember last night's peace
and us watching the always eventful nothing happening
as the light spilled from the poolroom of the hotel
and the players' movements went like fiddlers' elbows,
remember how now and then one person,
sometimes joined by another, then another
might linger by the back door with a smoke
and how – till it got too dark –
you could see the laughter you were far too far away to hear.

2 Some Things I Covet in Jura Lodge

(even though my Tom finds them just a wee bit too much)

that fearsomely fantastical
armchair upstairs made entirely of antlers and deerhide like
 something out of Cocteau's *La Belle et la Bête*
the tinpot suit of armour
the little green chipped 1940s kitchen chairs
the lobster creel for a lampshade
the pink teacup the typewriter the old black phone
the old scuffed leather sofa the red Paisley throw
the floral lining of the Edwardian cabin trunk in the Rose Room
the Mozart-printed cushions in the Music Room
that big mad portrait in the Portrait Room
of some little plumed Lord Fauntleroy riding on a goat!
the tall French mirror in the Portrait Room
the huge shell in the White Room
the bluebirds
on the glass fingerplate in the Bluebird Room
the tipsy wooden seagull
on the bedside table in the Bluebird Room
the Victorian ladies' hunting jacket
the American Folk Art hangers with the heart-shaped cut-outs
the tall window in the hall
on the blue wall
with the perfectly framed view of one of the Paps

3 Cornucopia

Darling, it is your birthday.
This would be the twentieth we have woken up to together
– except last year you were in hospital
and I woke alone at home early in our empty wide bed
thinking of you a mile away in that
bleak narrow one with the hospital corners.

Today I woke first – the sun so bright it almost hurt
streaming in through that swathe of white linen at the window
and, picture of health, your head on the pillow
ablaze in its storm of grey curls I love.
Caught the sun, caught the sun, my love,
didn't you, yesterday
on our first full day on the Isle of Jura?

Was it late in the afternoon, exposed on that
clifftop walk we took from above the Ferry at Feolin past
Sailor's Grave towards Inver and the ruins of Cnocbreac?
Was it earlier in the deceptively dappled light
on the walk to Jura House Garden?
On the shore path at Ardfin, where the
fuschia flared and the flagrant rhododendrons blossomed
along the loud banks of the Abhainn Beag Burn?
Was it when we took our picnic of
oatcakes and cheese and apple and lay in the sun
against the rocks at Traigh Bhan, the White Beach,
where those five blonde, tall
teenage lads, down from the Big House, no doubt,
were splashing and shouting in the surf till they
ran out, shaking themselves like dogs, laughing,
then paused to pass a pleasant time of day with such
impeccable public-school good manners
it was almost parodic?
Was it when, alone again on the empty beach,
we squinted into the sun
and looked for Heather Island and the ruined castle, argued

whether in the distance
what we could see was Arran, Kintyre or Ireland
and you were trying to persuade me that
it might just be worth it to brave the water's cold?
Or did we catch too much sun later
in the blaze of the gardens,
among the astonishing arches, barbered slopes
and walled gardens of exuberant exotica?
Was it when I lingered in the shade of the sheds
selecting us each an artichoke for supper,
till, leaving the money in the trustbox,
I came out into the sun again to
see you with Peter Cool, the gardener,
who was showing you, cupped in his hand, that
perfect-looking house-martin that somehow could not fly?

No, I think we burned up
as we were drawing by the tea-tent,
you and I facing in different directions
and so engrossed in what we were doing
we didn't notice time passing or the sun beating down
or those so cheeky chaffinches sneaking under
the paper napkins to steal our lemon cake.
Yes, we must have spent an hour, more,
you with your big blue A3 sketchbook, I with my green.
Your choice (outward) was wild meadow, trees, sky, sea
mine, didn't know why, simply the tea-tent.
Was it that in my mind sang out the first line
of the sonnet *She is as in a field a silken tent*?
Was it the cool dark of its interior, taut ropes,
the festive arabesques of its tent-white roof
against the intricate sky?
The swipe of its bonny blue awning?

Was it my longing to
loop across the page with blue those scalloped edges
and dot the tall swathes of long grass and wildflower
with poppies, kingcups, dandelions and something blue?

I remember when it was time to pack up you said,
OK, a challenge, five minutes, we change sides
and draw the other person's view and,
as it happened,
in five minutes
you caught more than I had in that whole hour.

Wake up, my twenty-years' love, and see
how many things can happen
today, for
that whisky we had a nip of last night had already
made it to its bourbon cask for ageing
when your Dionysus curls were black as grapes
and I buried my face in them on the
first
of the lovely,
finite
birthdays we'll have together.

Wake up, wake up
in this ridiculous room with
the huge shell bigger than a basin on the chest of drawers
for this is a house of many concetti
and here where we sleep
the motifs
are the coral and the scallop and the conch,
a mollusc multitude
of small shells that are cockles whorls and spirals
tiny dishes of mother of pearl and unicorn horns all
spilling from the ceiling's chandelier
like grapes from a cornucopia.
So wake up, won't you,
and enjoy being us
inside the shell of this morning here in the White Room?
In the bleached light the only colour
your old blue tee-shirt over the back of the basket chair
and the mottled, bottled shells
in those glass jars beside that great pile of blue-grey, slate-grey,

sea-washed pebbles
making a raised beach of the mantelpiece.

The big deep roll-top bath that stands in this bedroom
is the biggest and shiniest shell of all,
its inside so new it's nacreous.
Oh, I'm going to let the
Buck's Fizz we always have on birthday breakfasts
spill over
as I lie up to my neck in bubbles,
swigging it, be the
oldest, plumpest, homeliest, happiest,
most shameless Aphrodite on the half shell –
white curtains wide open
to the astonishing un-Scottish sun and the dazzling sea
and you, my love,
sprawled across the bed opposite
talking to me and opening your presents.

Word in your shell-like, sweetheart,
wake up!
With your birthday
a whole day
a holiday
before us.

4 No Excuse, But Honestly

it's hard to draw
Jura's beauty –
foxgloves and fuchsia far too flashy for
just black and white
hard to write –
the mountains with their purple passages
the long curve of empty road
the wide swathe of empty moor
the too-blue-for-Scotland sky
this
intricacy of thistles
far too intent on being emblematic

5 Legacy

Scribbled in my Jura notebook:

here the willow is called the sallow
today we saw an adder its
arrow markings + that slither-under also
a pair of eagles up near Three Arched Bridge v.
big – the 1st rose up from long grass with smthng in its talons
J
U
R
A
written so
long & thin up & down the lovely shape of it on tht old map
there are 2 brand-new crofthouses at Ardfernal and Knockrome
and Gwen the busdriver is v. happy (new
children for the school) thanx 2 Crfting Commission
Tarbert Inverlussa Lowlandman's Bay
Barnhill Orwell E. Blair TB motorbike 1984
Corrievrechan? (sp?)
Corryvreakan?
Corryvreckan (!)
Cauldron of Breakan (superstition) Devil's washing tub
Wow!!!! Corryvreckan really whirls well worth the
long shoogle in Landrover + the climb
loaded pleasure boats so far below
come out from Crinan to dare Corryvreckan
I wouldn't!
Corran Sands so wide and empty xcept fr
tht one wee boy in a red sunhat with hs spade
Corran Sands yes – Scotland! – swam (not cold!)
Shy red-haired lad at Friday Ceildh fantastc dancer (best)
6,500 deer 170 people (cull Autmn annual)
Craighouse Dstillry palmtrees hotel
Bay of Small Isles
Small Isles Bay
squat lobster tails delish – @ hotel (birthday dinner)

deer so many herds so close U see
the velvet on their antlers calm as cattle cropping grass
wot abt those ducks! Mergansers? Eiders?
Came def. conversing – cos we heard them –
flock of 12 from out at sea somewhere in to pier
then simult. all dive –
under fr ages!
every 1 xcept 1 bck up with 1 pink fish in beak
distillery tour Margaret (Michael's wife Islay orig.)
peat-reek barley smoky air
grist mash tun wort hopper
mill maltster 20 thousand litres of water
(Market Loch) maun yeast sugars
copper stills lantern or half-ball stills
feints 'low-wines' the foreshots and the tails
20 millings a wk
20 maltings
10 washbacks
not whsky unless oak cask in Scotland minimum 3years
sherry butts Spain (oloroso)
Isle of Jura aged in Bourbon Casks
brought frm far America & charred inside
88 degrees 78% alcohol
Tom saw an otter up close & swimming
down by the ferry Sat. jst as we were leaving

In my sketchbook:

Monday: clouds, clouds, Tom (profile)
Tuesday: tea tent at Ardfin Gardens, quick calligraphic landscape
Wednesday: Camas an Staca – Standing Stone/ sheep/ Islay ferry
Thursday: nothing (Corryvreckan trip, Land Rover then long trek)
Friday: the wee boy in the red hat
UL72 the blue boat (best –
yet at the time felt just wasn't working)
and from the pier-end in black and white
Craighouse stretched out
underneath

the Paps
and
home with
in the winter
a nip
of Legacy to sip.

Note: during the extraordinarily fine July of 2006, my husband Tom and I had the great good fortune to be – as guests of a Scottish Book Trust writer-in-residence scheme – the very first people to sleep in the brand-new, bonny and baroque (just designed and redecorated 'by the Paris interior decorator Bambi Sloan', it said) Jura Lodge, where we spent five days and nights, handselling it.

Lavender's Blue

in memory of Adrian Mitchell

First of April, old friend,
best of friends
and you are three months dead.
Fool's Day and I wish you'd jump up and
shout *huntigowk!* and it
would turn out to be the cruelest joke.
But no, it's true – 2009, and you'd have none of it,
three months and this whole bloody
turning world
has piled new atrocities and lies on old
– Gaza's latest hell happened
without you to sing the song
of simple *this is wrong*

You're gone
and, boy, we're going to miss you

So
I'm out in the new April sunshine of Sauchiehall Street
buying the best two books of nursery rhymes
for two brand-new babies – thinking of you
not dead
any more than the *other* Adrian
or Burns or Byron or Bix – yes,
there you go, chewing the fat with John Keats
walking Daisy the Dog of Peace
on Hampstead Heath

Boys and girls come out to play
The moon doth shine as bright as day –
Now there's too little action,
Too much talk:
When the bottle's open,
Throw away the cork –

Your books ain't on my bookshelves,
But in my heart and on my kitchen table
And you tell me to just sing my own silly songs
As well as I am able.

The Optimistic Sound

in memory of Michael Marra

'I'd wheel my wheelbarrow up Kilimanjaro' – from the Michael Marra song, 'If Dundee Was Africa'

'Make the optimistic sound' – from the Michael Marra song, 'Like Another Rolling Stone'

Today
one of the hundreds of friends at your funeral
was just desperate to tell me the story of when he first met you,

'Michael just came on, sat down at the piano,
started singing and och! . . .
anyway, after he was finished and we were
standing together in the wings, well,
I was that over the moon I was
jist gittering on and on I was, about how
knocked out I was, and here onstage the orchestra
had started and he was quite entitled
to tell me to shut it, anybody else
would have just said *shut up!* – it was called for –
but no, he just puts his finger to his lip, says
ssh! so soft you could hardly hear him and one word, whispered:
listen.
That was Michael.'

This morning Marianne and James and I
drove past your house around the corner.
Drawn curtains, and
I thought of Peggy pressing her good black clothes, Alice
bringing her a strong hot cup of tea I hoped, Matthew
mibbe polishing everybody's shoes, and we
went on to where you

went every day you were at home
to see the ospreys.

October's end and an empty nest.
That big bunchy structure of sticks and moss not
ramshackle in the least but
firm, safe as houses in the high winds,
not perched but planted,
strong and wild and grand as the absent birds themselves
on top of its high pylon, a nest
returned to every year for decades now,
a local secret easily visible from the long straight road
bordered in tall trees and this year's
extra braw show of bright autumn colour.
In a line of pylons striding across a flat plain field
in farmland in Angus, that one flat top
crowned by the ospreys' nest,
and, in the electric air,
all around the slow leaves falling.

Michael,
how proud you were – most years –
if you were home – to witness the young ones' maiden flight,
how determined this year not to miss it.

And there was silence, Michael.
Not even a whisper of rustling leaves,
the wind dropped and just one great leaf took an age
to come spiralling to the ground in
perfect silence.
Till suddenly a honking and a ragged vee of urgent birds,
wings beating in double time, forming and
reforming as they went their
flock-perfect travelling shape as best they could as
they crossed the wide sky above the ospreys' nest in no time
and I don't know if it was an optimistic sound or not
but anyway it was the sound of being alive, and they were making it.
Wild geese

coming back from their far cold wherever
to winter here
as if they were ospreys
and Angus was Africa.

Wedding Vow: The Simplest, Hardest and the Truest Thing

a dialogue to speak

One: We live in love, so finally are come today
(beyond the gladrags and the sweet bouquet
beyond cake or ring or all this fuss)
to this, the simplest and the truest thing for us.

Other: If you can say, my love – and hand on heart –
I will love you until death do us part –

One: Hand on heart,
I will love you till death do us part.

Other: Then look me in my eyes – and now!
and here! – this kiss we kiss shall be our vow.

Written as part of a series of vows for weddings and partnerships, commissioned by Carol Ann Duffy for the Guardian *on the occasion of the Royal Wedding, 29 April 2011.*

Anniversaries

for Sophie Logan and Vas Piyasena on your wedding day

By the time, a year from now,
when the anniversary is 'paper'
you'll have been, I reckon, Vas and Sophie,
the best part of a dozen years together.

On your Wooden Wedding – isn't that five? –
wee Sonny will be a seasoned schoolboy already
and 'Mr & Mrs', those
lovely, ordinary words 'my wife', 'my husband'
long, long so habitual by then that –
even though you've long been
lovers, partners, are *parents* now and will be
each other's best friend forever –
are words that sound so new and strange,
words to be lump-in-the-throat proud of today.
After the grown-up, take-a-deep-breath, 'I do', 'I do'
what can you say?

'My wife', 'my husband', that's what!
And when, paper, cotton, linen – I forget the order –
roll around remember,
whether (ruby, silver) they seem to call for
flowers, something precious, or (wood, iron, steel)
a thing as plain prosaic as new utensils
they neither mark accurately the years together nor
can they begin to list what marriage is made of.

May that be dailiness – and delight in it,
sunsets sometimes, full moons,
music, moments, meals, long sleeps curled like spoons
together, your children, hard work, holidays,
home, laughter, friends and family,
love always.

A Cambric Shirt

for Gordon and Camrie Maclean (father and daughter)

Because the sound of his daughter's name
was as soft to him as the cloth it was,
in Scots, the auld word for – *camrie* – chambray,
a cambric shirt was what that day
he wore to her wedding.
And it was
the two of them alone knew the why of it.

Because he'd hap her up forever in the love
that, light in his heart, let her go to the good man
any father would be glad to see his lassie
married onto, this was atween them baith
one small secret hanselling: a cambric shirt

the shirt he'd have gien aff his back for her,
would still without the asking, *the coat so warm*
when the rivers freeze and *the snowflakes storm*
to keep her from the howling winds,
his *plaidie to every angry airt*
he'd shelter her
hap her weel-clad
in the cauld blast
in the cauld blast

his father-love
the camrie sark
withoot ony seam or needlewark.

The Light Comes Back

In the Mid-Midwinter

after John Donne's 'A Nocturnal on St Lucy's Day'

At midday on the year's midnight
into my mind came
I saw the new moon late yestreen
wi the auld moon in her airms
though, no,
there is no moon of course –
there's nothing very much of anything to speak of
in the sky except a gey dreich greyness
rain-laden over Glasgow and today
there is the very least of even this for us to get
but
the light comes back
the light always comes back
and this begins tomorrow with
however many minutes more of sun and serotonin.

Meanwhile
there will be the winter moon for us to love the longest,
fat in the frosty sky among the sharpest stars,
and lines of old songs we can't remember
why we know
or when first we heard them
will aye come back
once in a blue moon to us
unbidden

and bless us with their long-travelled light.

Autumn with Magpie, Pomegranate

this morning
a cruel curve of black-patent beak,
a single terrifying eye
at my high window looking in –
the cocky, glossy bulk
of that big blue-black and white bird,
its gleam, its stare –
and I thought of Robert Lowell's skunk
that would not scare

but out in the gold of this October afternoon
caught in a sudden swirl of leaves
I think *Corryvreckan*,
but tell myself we're still very far
from winter's washing tub
and yes here I am
happed up warm and
out to buy whichever Halloween cake in the
baker's window is putting the best face on it,
here I am
with a pomegranate in my pocket
like a bomb packed with garnets.

a pomegranate,
its scarred and shiny rind
both buff and blebbed with russet like
this air which rustles, crackles.

I think
late beauty is the best beauty as
un-saluted
but with a hop skip and a jump in front of me
today's tally of magpies
flips from *one for sorrow* to
two for joy.

Beyond It

a 'Golden Shovel' poem

In seas. In windsweep. They were black and loud. – Gwendolyn Brooks

The bad weather is trying to get in,
so veils of rain become blatterings, seas
over-arch, they pound and rake our shores. In
they come – far, far beyond the high-tide mark with windsweep
and drag, splintering all they suck back in. They
make a nothing of all things that once were
our all-in-all, stood proud. The skies go black
with thick murk, this impenetrable cloud, and
more-than-weather stirs one boiling broth of chaos, irresistible
    and loud.

How to Be the Perfect Romantic Poet

Be born male.
Begin your career as a poet early.
Take advantage of your nursemaid's momentary distraction
by – not yet a twelvemonth –
crawling to the fire and snatching out a live coal, flamed
and glowing, learning
to brand Promethean sensation to your flesh and brain.
(This will also initiate you nicely into the twin satisfactions
of rousing the whole household with your shrieking
and getting a maid into trouble.)

Be orphaned ere you grow to double figures.
Ever after, idolise your father, disappoint your mother.
Have a sister (every Romantic poet worth his salt most certainly
has a sister). She'll be the one to hearken when you sing
Then come my Sister! come, I pray,
With speed put on your woodland dress;
And bring no book: for this one day
We'll give to idleness.

Even if you are not Lord Byron
be mad and bad and dangerous to know.

Be faithful to your Muse and marry the wrong woman.
Your Muse will most fulsomely reward you.

When in London, lodge at the Salutation and Cat,
that hotbed of sedition. Thrill to that.

Leave your long black hair unpowdered,
wear your blue topcoat with a white swansdown waistcoat,
your mudded stockings most spectacularly bespattered – but
most vehemently refuse to change them just to please your wife.

Dream, but
ere you're older (if you want to get much older)
attempt
to wean yourself off your predilection for laudanum, opium,
    brandy,
drop the Kendal Black Drop for the more sedative stimulants
of egg-nog and Oronoko tobacco.
Soar,
escape the real world of gruel, sulphur-ointment, haberdashery,
pig-iron, cotton manufactories and silk mills;
worship all winged creatures – Angels, Harpies,
the starling, sea-mew, ostrich, owl, canary, vulture,
the nightingale, sparrow, thrush, bustard, tom-tit, dove, duck,
    linnet, lark
and, ah,
the albatross . . .

Dread, above all, becalming, stasis.
Love the wild wave,
the humble bird-limed thornbush; let nature be your teacher
but be *a library cormorant*, dive deep.
When it thunders
run bareheaded, harebrained, out into the rain.
Miss all deadlines – write all night,
tempt and court the Nightmare and the Succubus
in pursuit of the green radiance,
in pursuit of the fugitive colours of the day.

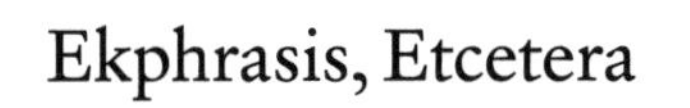
Ekphrasis, Etcetera

Photograph, Art Student, Female, Working Class, 1966

Her hair is cut into that perfect slant –
An innovation circa '64 by Vidal Sassoon.
She's wearing C&A's best effort at Quant
Ending just below the knicker-line, daisy-strewn.
Keeping herself in tights could blow her grant
Entirely, so each precious pair is soon
Spattered with nail varnish dots that stop each run.
She's a girl, eighteen – just wants to have fun.

She's not 'a chick'. Not yet. Besides, by then
She'll find the term 'offensive'. 'Dollybird' to quote
Her favourite mags, is what she aspires to when
Her head's still full of *Honey* and *Petticoat*.
It's almost the last year that, quite this blithely, men
Up ladders or on building sites wolf-whistle to note
The approval they're sure she will appreciate.
Why not? She did it for *their* benefit, looks great.

Nor does she object. Wouldn't think she has the right.
Though when that lech of a lecturer comments on her tits
To a male classmate, openly, she might
Feel – quick as a run in nylon – that it's
Not what ought to happen, is *not polite*,
She'll burn, but smile, have no word that fits
The insult, can't subject it to language's prism.
In sixty-six there's plenty sex, but not 'sexism'.

Soon: *The Female Eunuch* and enough
Will be enough. Thanks to newfound feminism and Greer
Women'll have the words for all this stuff,
What already rankles, but confuses her, will seem clear
And she'll (consciously) be no one's 'bit of fluff'
Or 'skirt' or 'crumpet'. She'll know the rule is 'gay' not 'queer',
'Ms' not 'Miss' or 'Mrs' – she'll happily obey it
And, sure as the Pill in her pocket, that's how she'll say it.

This photo's saying nothing, is black and white, opaque.
A frozen moment, not a memory.
The boyfriend with the Pentax took it for the sake
Of taking it, a shot among many others, randomly,
To see how it would develop. Didn't imagine it'd make
An image so typical it'd capture time so perfectly.
How does she feel? Hey, girl, did it feel strange
To be waiting for the a-changing times to change?

Some Old Photographs

Weather evocative as old-fashioned scent

the romance of dark stormclouds
in big skies over the low wide river,
                              of long shadows and longer shafts of light

of smoke,
   fabulous film-noir stills of Central Station,
of freezing fog silvering the chilled, stilled parks
   of the glamorous past
   where drops on a rainmate are sequins
   under the streetlight, in the black and white

your young, still-lovely mother laughs, the
hem of her sundress whipped up
by a wind on a beach
somewhere doon the watter
before you were even born

all the Dads in hats
are making for Central at five past five
in the snow, in the rain, in the sudden *what-a-scorcher*,
in the smog, their
belted dark overcoats white-spattered by the starlings

starlings swarming
in that perfect and permanent cloud
above what was
never really this photograph
but always all the passing now
and noise and stink and smoky breath of George Square

wee boays, a duchess, bunting, there's a
big launch on the Clyde
and that boat is yet to sail

‘The Scullery Maid’ and ‘The Cellar Boy’ by Jean-Baptiste-Siméon Chardin

I The scullery maid speaks:

He liked me fine, the Master,
called me ‘pretty as a picture’
the day he stopped me at my scouring.
I was more than a mere scullery maid to him he said –
or rather as something to pay attention to today
than a bonny scullery maid like me
he could think of nothing better.
He never called me by my name – I think he never knew it,
or needed to – nor so much as touched my rough-work apron
that he said had a coarseness he liked the look of
as so he did my good clean house-frock’s unbleached
nothing-sort-of-colour that set off nicely
the peach-ness of my skin.
That got me blushing, but I needn’t have bothered.
Looking back, I can see his glad eye
was as greedy for copper, earthenware, old cooperage,
the glimmer in the long-handled pan I worked at.
He made every bit as much of that daft cellar boy
who is the bane of my life always with his crude remarks
and grabbing hands given the half-a-chance I aye
have to make sure he never gets. The Master
made him look human, almost handsome, yes,
he certainly stands out there in his kitchen-whites
against the cellar’s dimness beside the old tub
among his jugs and flask and funnel.
To him we were a pair.

‘Hold still!’ he said and that was the only time
he ever spoke to me with any hint of sharpness.
And I might have said, ‘Never mind, M’sieur Chardin,
that I’ve work to be done the mistress won’t be letting me off with
and these pots won’t wash themselves!’ – except it wasn’t

my place to, was it?
Besides, squinting at me through those spectacles,
dabbing at his canvas, tutting,
I could see that he was hard at work
and I liked that.
It gave me pause.

2 The cellar boy speaks:

He's no wi the toun at aw, the Maister.
He's in a warld o his ain, plooterin
Wi paint on cloth stretched roon wid frames, footerin
Wi crayons, burnt twigs o charcoal, broken chalks, in a slaister
Amang the thick oil-stink o linseed, the sherp sting
O turpentine, gum arabic, white spirit. Pride o place
Aye to the palette an the easel staunin tall aboon the mess
That the maid got a richt flea-in-her-ear for tidying.

First day he drew me? Whit maist I mind
Is thon rat cook's terrier stertit-up from oot the coarner stour.
Chased fur its life, it leapt richt ower the Maister's fit
But he peyed nae tent to it. Never even seen it – blind
Tae awthin but the task in haun, he never heard the poor
Rat's last heich, sair squeal nor the snarlin o the dug eftir it.

Somethin o thon stubborn terrier in him.
Noo his dander was up the hunt was on
And he had nae choice but to get me doon.
He had me in his sights, his thumb
Oot at airm's length like he was pressin in a tack
Nailing me to nuthin. He lukked at me. I lukked back.
He's never liked me. That day he couldnae get enough
Till his tea was cauld and the Mistress in the huff.

Specs on his neb's end, een screwed up, squintin, he
Was eftir something – whit I dinna ken – in me.

The Art of Willie Rodger

is *essential* essentially

it's   made by hand   created from the heart
from the heart of this most creative family

with perfect   and perfected   economy
with nothing but
the eye   the cut
the dab hand
the knife   the lino, ink and roller
the perfect paper (the black and
not *quite*
white?)
with maybe the black on softest red?   the black on buff?
with the never too much   the always enough
the dab hand
the either/or
the both, the and

with   essentially
the block and the roller   the paper
the ink
its light, deep
funny, sad
per-
jink

who
in a print   can make Scottish *haiku*?

Willie

sees
and what he sees *shows* face to face

it's full of grace

A Man Nearly Falling in Love

after the linocut by Willie Rodger

no one is more dangerous
no one
than the man nearly falling in love
his eye gone from glad-eye to gaga
his mouth open in an *oh no!*

get him
plucking out
that arrow which
almost
pierced him in the heart and
where it hurts.

he's floored   temporarily
he's fallen
for someone   almost
fallen for her but
not
in love no
not exactly.

lethal.

someone   he'll make sure of it
someone
will have to suffer for this.

In Alan Davie's Paintings

An ee
an open ee
whit seems but an ashet o
bools and penny-cookies mak an arabesque
an arra-heid edder frae ablow it
gaes serpent-slinkan
yont the picture frame.
a jazz o bird-heids, herts, peeries, playin cairts
the crescent mune –
a the shapes and symbols frae
ankh to ziggurat, corbie-steppit.
whiles a rattle-stane blatter
whiles a hurly-gush o colour –
this lovely lowe o cramasie, soy-saft,
noo the reid, reid, reid o thunnercups,
a braid and tappietourie swag o emerant
yallochie
blae.

Three Stanzas for Charles Rennie Mackintosh

on the centenary of the opening of the great architect's building for the Glasgow School of Art, 15 December 2009

I

'It is but a plain building that is required.'
North light, set dimensions for studios, that budget inspired,
In no way constrained, you. Dear Ghost, Dear Genius,
A plain wonder of a building's what you gave to us.
Volume, light, line, astonishing rhythms of space,
Guts, harmony, surprises, *seemliness*, a great place
To work in, learn in, live in, take for granted.
Much more than they ever knew they wanted
Was what you gave Fra Newbery, the Governors, the World, the
    Future –
Changing for ever the possibilities of architecture.
A prime modernist squarely in the Scotch Baronial tradition
And proud of it! Definitively beyond definition.
Your details delight us endlessly with their endless variation –
Always decorated construction, never constructed decoration.

II

'Art is the flower,' you said, 'Life is the green leaf'.
Time is the judge. Time is the thief.

III

Die Hoffnung ist – graphic, 1901.
Wee motif: the blaeberry of the Mackintosh Clan.
The other? Abstracted, a sprig of heather for your Margaret.
There is hope lettered in your own alphabet –
Blaeberry and heather twinned in that symbolism you devised.
So what if that motto you made your own was plagiarised?
There is hope – yes – in honest error, none
In the mere stylist's icy perfection.

Labyrinth

for the students of the Glasgow School of Art

'first you have to know the rules to break them'
not so   the artist says:
first you have to know there are no rules
not to break is
first
to know no rules
except

the unbreakable rules of the
call it your
'art'   or 'truth'   or 'muse'   or 'process'
the goddess accident
as she   very deliberately
shows you what you want to do

and exactly the rules you must first invent then
slavishly obey

this time   and this time only

it's as if Ariadne handed you the
tentative end of a ball of twine and now you know
the creature   and all creation
is   it really is
down there for you to get
                    for you can smell it

smoke or musk or dung   a reek of danger
most definitely danger

one good student tells testifies:
my art was once all about my dreams but my
dreams made no sense to anyone but me so
I started to explore caves
real caves with real paint
the exact spaces between
the walls and the
rule was it had to be real exactly as-was and the
intervals precise and the

more real I got the more people told me
my art was like their dreams

Email to Alastair Cook

Thanks for sharing those images
from the Imperial War Museum website –
nine or ten photographs of
Greenock women in the Great War
working in the sugar sheds.

When their men were in the trenches
they were welcomed in the workplace
for the duration
to work their fingers to the bone
then, after that shift's overtime was over,
keep the home-fires burning too.
Hard labour
but these photos show they sort of liked it? –
see them, what are they like, eh? –
skirts kilted thigh-high as they lug those sacks
of raw molasses to or from the hook and hoist
or paddle barefoot, shouldering heavy shovels,
up to their knees in those
great mounds and drifts of sugar,
white bings, shifting the stuff in jigtime to
the bagging room.
Strong women,
solid, archetypal as Millet's gleaners
or Degas's laundresses,
queens of the sweet heaps,
singing their white-woman's blues.

And their voices were not refined.

They'd breenge brass-necked and raucous
through the toun streets at lowsin time,
pay-packets in their pockets, sure that
once this War was over
they'd no be sent hame and telt they'd better

learn to mak a guid pot o soup.
On another day – a black yin –
when Mairn and Mysie baith get their telegrams, they'll
greet wi them, greet sair, then rally round
and bear them up, but today
they're no feart! –
they're laughing as they brag out loud
about the legendary bandy-leggit Betty
who could smuggle oot three pokes in each leg o her bloomers
    above the extra-strong elastic –
and nane o whose neighbours would ever
go short o a spoonfu to sweeten their tea.

Alastair, tomorrow
I'll meet you at Central, eh? And we'll go down together
to where the river widens and goes silver
and I'll see
what you and Alec and Annie and the other artists
have made of this a century later,
have made of those spaces rendered lovely,
rendered elegiac with disuse.

To enter one of your photographs
is to be in the presence of absence,
to be humbled,
to be where even the light is granulated
and the layered shadows seem to retain traces
of that burnt sugar smell.
And it's as if your open lens
wasn't only looking but was
listening for the traces –
Alastair, your glad eye for
the spaces and those places
make those absent voices
sing.

The Ballad of Elsie Inglis

I

1864. Elsie Maud Inglis, in India
Was born, seventh child, favourite daughter
Of a most enlightened father –
Despite his being a servant of the Empire,
Of the Raj and Queen Victoria.

Wee Elsie wanted to cure the whole wide world.
Blotches big and red as poppies
Were the pockmarks and the mock-measles
That she painted on her dollies.

Daily she washed off the paint
From the dollies' faces,
Daily she disinfected the dollies
In all the dollies wounded places.
Daily she tended to her dollies,
Daily the dollies got better.
Elsie's (gentle) mother and Elsie's (just) father
Had nothing but kisses and yeses
When Elsie told them, 'I am going to be a doctor'.

1886. Grown-up, back in Scotland,
Soon as her medical training began
Elsie knew she had it in her to be a surgeon
As good as any man.
And many a suffering woman
Would most certainly prefer
(If it came to baring her all beneath the surgeon's knife)
Said knife be wielded by her.

They had to thole tyrannical husbands –
His property, in law – that was a wife.
He'd the right to refuse her an operation –
Even one to save her life.

Surely everyone saw what Elsie saw?
'Twould be only common decency
To have female specialists in obstetrics,
Paediatrics and gynaecology?

1894. Doctor Elsie Inglis founded in Edinburgh
A Women's Hospital for the Poor.
1914. Somebody shot somebody in Sarajevo
And the whole bloody world was at war.

1914. *Britain Needs You!* and
Young, green, lads were queueing up to enlist.
Elsie Inglis saw the necessity
For the doctor she was, for the suffragist –

For patriotic Elsie knew she could muster
All-female medical teams who would want
Just as if they were fighting soldiers,
To be risking their lives at the front.

Then the injustice of further denying women the vote
Would be more than crystal clear.
So off to the Castle, to the RAMC,
Went Elsie to volunteer.

The man from the War Office smiled at Elsie
My good lady, go home and sit still.
Did this make Elsie Inglis angry?
If it did, it was grist to her mill

For Elsie smiled back at the man, said nothing.
She really did not want to be rude.
Thought: If my government doesn't want Women's Field Hospitals
Surely some other government would?

2

My good lady, go home and sit still.
But she did not, would not, could not, could she,
take no for an answer?
She was almost fifty years old already, already ill
(Though she kept this close to her chest) with the cancer
She, and only in her last days, swearing her to secrecy,
Confided to Mary, that long-serving hospital-cook she trusted,
She had a . . . *certain malignancy*
She was sure she'd survive and not be bested
by. Oh, the pain it was truly chronic,
It really gave her what for,
And none of her nice nieces would ever get to ask her
Aunt Elsie, what did you do in the war?

But all this was 1917
And after three long years of that terrible War
Throughout which Elsie'd always known
Exactly what she was fighting
And what she was fighting for.

3

Her father's daughter –
She'd never minded this, just taken it for the compliment
She knew whoever had come out with it
Certainly meant it to be.
But, Edinburgh Castle, the War Office,
1914, that buffoon in charge of the RAMC . . . !
Elsie was not *his*, nor what he would call
Either a *lady* or *good.*
That she'd have to get round this damnable obstacle
Elsie well understood.

Written for the John Bellany and the Scottish Women's Hospitals Exhibition, 2016.

Gallimaufry

for the re-opening of Glasgow's Kelvingrove Art Gallery in July 2006

I

thon
big gink
that skinnymalink
giraffe
– the round-shouldered knock-kneed giraffe
with its half-daft embarrassed bug-eyed face-of-an-alien
and its *square spots* for godsake! – oh
ho you
better duck   giraffe   because watch!
a Spitfire's coming over

and has, just new,
swooped through
(very nearly scraping the balconies on either side and
taking the whole place down with it)
hangs fire in mid air
more brazen than the ten pendent electroliers
and almost as brilliantly
engineered as the seagull that flies beneath it

here's a hero for us
Spitfire –
your matt drab dark green khaki emblazoned LA198
each badged wing making an
OK-I-double-dare-you mockery of a target
with those insignia roundels of red and blue
we could almost touch your wingtips
can't but
contemplate how very skinny the snakehips of the
young men in the myth   in the history
who had to lift the lid and shimmy into your fateful cockpit

we can't but marvel
at the precision of the six guns of your cannon
and the five blades of your propeller

2

the smogs of the fifties   the emanations of old raincoats
a century of Capstan and cigars the
fusts and filth of the air factories bad
breath blitz and bombast that
tarry earl o hell *absolute black-mockitness*
made up of such a mixtermaxter as would make you dizzy
all that's
been just pure stripped from
this pale clean stone
in one miraculous
latex peel

so now I want to go there
take my nephew
say Davie you were only seven the
last time we could lift you up to
look into the glazed eye of Sir Roger the Elephant
and now you're ten and
it's three more years since the morning
his keeper gave breakfast
to that wrinkled and cynical as a general old veteran of
the Scottish Zoo and Variety Circus –
then handed him over
to *several soldiers and a man with an elephant gun*

Davie, I want to show you
the bones of the Baron of Buchlyvie
and his two horse shoes   Benin bronzes
the biggest spider and the smallest pygmy shrew
teach you all the names of the birds you can see in your garden
goggle with you at the fabulous skeleton of the giant Irish deer

at the ceratosaur the chiffchaff the willow warbler
the ebonised writing desk by Mackintosh that holds open its doors
like a Japanese lady holding out her arms in a kimono
show you amulets scarabs and talismans
the eye of Horus
and the hand of Fatima
show you the clouded leopard,
the dogsteeth necklace
the head of the Endrick Pike
fossils as lucid as the blueprint photograms of Anna Atkins
the mandrill
the masks of Menander
the La Faruk Madonna
the eyewitness watercolours of Auschwitz by Marianne Grant
the orrery and the beaded and birchbank souvenirs for tourists
made by the Metis and the Cree
show you
the King Billy banner from the Orange Lodge
the Statue of St Patrick say *sectarianism is history*
show you that Cezanne say
how do you like them apples
show you the bright and savage
Joan Eardley weans in the picture queue
– and Stanley Spencer's
tummeling their fatbum wulkies eternally around the railings
of *The Glen Port Glasgow*
I want you to keek back at that tousle-headed man
keeking out at you
at the snow
from *Windows in the West*
I want you to hear the *orchestrion* giving it laldy
and gawp at the Goliath birdeater that eats birds
I want us to wonder together
at the ptarmigan and the polecat and the Great Auk
and wonder why there are turnips engraved on the splendid
armour of the Earl of Pembroke,
I want to measure your height against the long legbone of the
giraffe,

say *hey*
Davie the last time you were up to here and
here!
now you're up to there

3

look at that gorgeous girl that
real Glasgow stoater done up to the nines
who is a perfect specimen of the present
if only we could preserve her

and she's gawping at that
very swanky perra black satin platforms
she says
haw lookit, lookit that toty wee perra peerie heels in see-thru plastic
made by Jean Rimbaud Paris in
nineteen fifty something,
jist gorgeous eh no?

come and I'll show you
the pretty tiny embroidered bootee
to cover the stump left by the work of the footbinder in China
the flamboyant neckties of Emilio Coia
in Italian silk
I'll show you the branks and the jougs and the nursing corset
the *ladies' silk safari suit*
and (tho she wore it to the opening a hundred years ago
it's still fresh as a daisy)
I'll show you the *bonny pink frock of the Duchess of Fife*

4

one man gave his wife
that peacock brooch in enamel on silver
another a bunch of fives
and *pit her to the branks*
stitched her up and banged her in that scold's bridle

what is the taste of iron on the tongue?
whit like is it?
and what are we like?

we are here
and there
and even that is neither here nor there because

this one is suddenly back in a Saturday in the sixties
walking with her Dad and
hearing the sound of the skelp of her brand-new sandals
on the marble floor

that one remembers
sitting *right there* next to Alasdair Gray at Miss Jean Irwin's
Saturday morning children's classes in the nineteen fifties
and *how he just had it, even then*

the lonely divorcee
looks at the beaded deerskin moccasins
the Native American hunting coat of sealskin reads
the designs a woman painted on her husband's coat
are guided by his dreams

there's a new widower in Egyptology
with a heavy heart –
an Orpheus among the faience and elegance
and he's studying the Book of the Dead
wishes he could *bathe in gazelle's milk*
the eye of Horus

wishes he could bring her back
look at
these lovers, these Sunday-afternoon lovers
beneath their flung-on clothes still naked
from their Saturday night and long Sunday morning
blink and stare at the suit of armour amazed
what could anyone want with armour?

well, ask the Temminck's pangolin, the
nine-banded armadillo, ask
the man in the seventeenth century who wore this
thick buff coat of elk hide with the
real blood and the bullet mark

Mammy, Mammy I want to go back to the diaroma
see the hare change its coat
winter to summer and back to white-and-magic winter again
I want to overhear somebody else's granddad explain
to that wee boy who isny even interested
the name of the device that makes it work is *Pepper's Ghost*

5

there should be a cliché that goes
as greedy as Glasgow –
glad-eyed Glasgow
that's aye grabbed its chances goodstyle, gone
loot from Lucknow?
oh aye, sees it
the emperor of China's cloak, seized from the Summer Palace?
aye, sees that
sees yon ghost dance shirt
they sent us from Lakota, Dakota
(OK it's a replacement) and
sees our jade
our gesso panels
our man in armour
our Orange Blind
sees our Noel Paton
sees our Avril Paton
our Salvador Dali

Glasgow flourish?
Oh aye no hauf oh
whit a
gallus gallimaufry!

let us haste to Kelvingrove . . .

Way Back in the Paleolithic

Long long ago
What do you know
Even back then
In them caves of Lascaux
More than thirty thousand years ago
Way back in pre-history
This was already the essential mystery:

Art, art, what is it for?
To bring into being what never existed before.

It's that elemental
Artistic vibe
That binds us together as part of the tribe –
Every father, mother, every sister, every brother
Every man and every woman
Needed them animals on the cave walls
To define themselves as human.

Art, art, what is it for?
To bring into being what never existed before.

Way, way back and long ago
In the caves of
Chauvet, Altamira, Lascaux
Those first folk –
Those first about-to-be artists – had to face
That blank wall only Nature so far had had a go at
Somehow put it in its place.

So they bravely turned their hand to it,
Stencilling in its outline with the spatter and the spark
Of the spat and blown pigment
That drew so clearly where their hands both were and weren't
And they made their mark – with Art!

Art, art, what was it for?
To bring into being what never existed before.

In the Cueva de las Manos,
In Chauvet, Altamira and Lascaux
Already this fundamental inclination
That drives pro creation
Forced those folk to fashion
Something beyond religion or ritual – Art!

Art, art, what was it for?
To bring into being what never existed before.

Fetishes of priapic phalluses,
Amulets of big-bellied round-hipped split-vulva-ed Venuses,
Objects of clay, bone, antler, stone
For they knew man could not
Should not
Live by meat alone.

No they were
Not just hunters tasked with bringing home the bacon
But artists
With a mammoth undertaking!

Images of aurochs, bulls and bison,
Ochres, oxides, charcoal, mineral pigments,
Fierce felines, fleet equines, bear and deer –
Made from the life
And from imagination's figments.

Because their truest impulse was
To *capture something*
Soon running wild on the walls were
Hordes of realer than real creatures
The torches in the firelight
Flickered into the first motion pictures.

Did they dance?
They danced themselves to trance.
How do we know?
Bone flutes we found, stone drumsticks tell us so.
In the firelight, in the cave, beyond
All the other ordinary passing glories,
Beyond the fugitive music and the stories –
On the walls
Their Immortal Art!

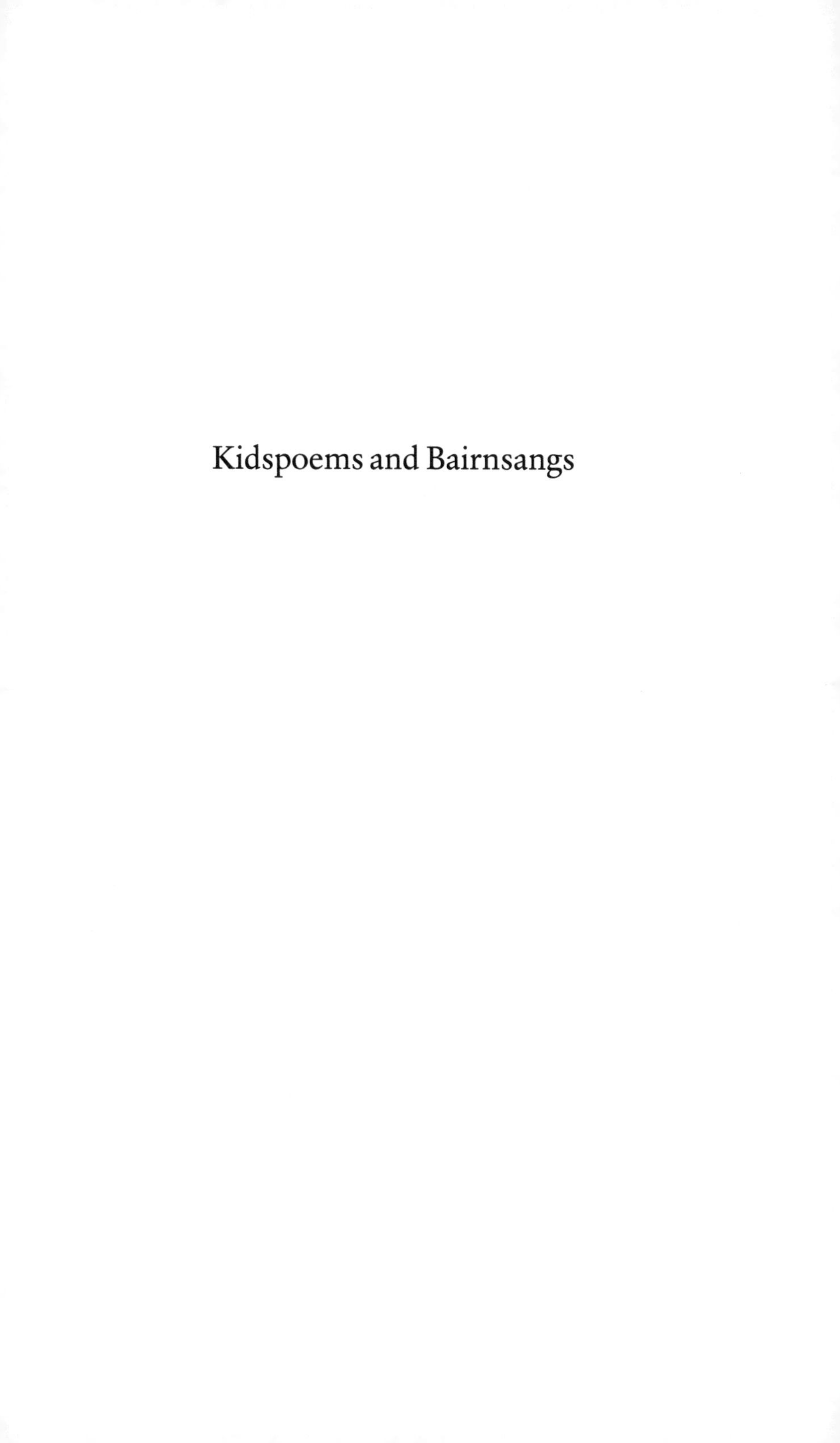

Kidspoems and Bairnsangs

How I'll Decorate My Tree

Written as a banner – with lines from London school children – for the Norwegian Christmas tree in Trafalgar Square, 2014.

It was still very far from Christmas
When my mamma said to me:
Tell me, Precious, what *you* going to hang
On *our* Christmas tree?

I said: the fairy-lights that Dad just fixed
And . . . jewel-coloured jelly-beans from the pick'n'mix –
Oh, and from it I'll dangle tinsel in tangles,
Sparkles, sequins and spangles,
A round golden coin (chocolate money),
That cracker joke that was *actually funny*,
My rosary beads – and a plastic rose
As red as Rudolph Reindeer's nose,
The gnome that grows the tangerines,
The picture of me with my tambourine,
And (this is Mum's favourite, she says)
The photo of all of us in our PJ's!
The Ladybird book that Lola lent me,
The blue butterfly bracelet that Brittany sent me,
The ear-ring I lost,
A pop-up Jack Frost,
A space-hopper, an everlasting gobstopper,
A pink-eyed sugar mouse,
The keys to my grandfather's house,
A tiny pair of trainers with silver laces,
And – now my smile is straight – gonna hang up my braces!
A marble, an angel-scrap, a star,
The very last sweetie out my advent calendar,
A kiss under the mistletoe,
A mitten still cracked with a crunch and a creak of snow,
That glitter scarf I finally got sick of,
A spoon with cake-mix still to lick off,

The Dove of Peace that our Darren made,
Some green thoughts in our tree's green shade –
I'll hang up every evergreen memory
Of moments as melted and gone
As that candle that was *supposed* to smell
Of cinnamon –
Memories big as a house and as small's
The baubles I used to call *ball-balls.*

With pleasure I'll treasure them
Then, on *proper* Christmas Day, I'll show them all to you
Between the Queen's Speech and Doctor Who.

Glasgow Nonsense Rhyme, Nursery Rhyme, for Molly

– who, fetched by her new parents, Graham and Julie, from distant Jiangxi province in China just in time for her first birthday, came home here to Glasgow

Molly Pin Li McLaren,
come home and look
at the pictures in your brand-new book –
a tree, a bird, a fish, a bell,
a bell, a fish, a tree, a bird.
Point, wee Molly, and say the word!

Oh Molly, I wish
you the moon as white and round as a dish
and a bell, a tree, a bird and a fish.

Touch! Taste! Look! Smell!
(tree, fish, bird, bell)
and listen, wee Molly, listen well
to the wind,
to the wind in the tree go swish
(bird, bell, tree, fish)
to the shrill of the bird and the plop of the fish
and the clang of the bell
and the stories they tell
the stories they tell,
Molly, the tree, the bird, the fish and the bell.

Glasgow's coat of arms has motifs of a tree, a bird, a fish and a bell, hence the traditional – this is the tree that never grew / this is the bird that never flew / this is the fish that never swam / this is the bell that never rang.

Nina's Song

Nina, come to Scotland
Nina come soon
We'll show you the wee-est field mouse
And the biggest, roundest moon.

The million-zillion stars'll *amaze* you –
So bright and so far . . .
Pick one and we'll sing you
Twinkle, twinkle little star

Come soon, Nina,
Come and never wonder why
There can be three perfect rainbows
In just one wide sky –

Just enjoy the bonny colours
Nina, never mind their names –
Although it's true
We will very much enjoy teaching you
Your *red, orange, yellow, green and blue*
Your *violet and indigo,*
And every colour that we know
Wee Nina, all the same.

And everything will be glad to see you
All the singing birds will go,
Nice to meet you, new wee Nina,
Hey, Nina – hello!

In Gaia's Poetry

Gaia does not care to rhyme.

She's right of course.
To start to put down words that end the same –
Soundwise – is to get on a horse
That's going to take you where you might not really want to go,
Make you say what you – maybe – didn't want to say?
Not be true to what you're writing
So
(As Truth's the Thing) *that*'d be no good, no way!

And Gaia's got a point – *except*
There's the fun of what you don't expect –
The *half*-rhymes, echoes, chimes,
The *internal* (inside a line) and unstressed rhymes
Where the sense doesn't end on the rhyme-word with a clunk.
There's the fun too of the thought you never would've thunk
Were it not for the rhyme that took you there.
There's the *couplet* (a new rhyme after every pair
Of lines – AABB), there's the interlaced *quatrain*
That goes ABAB, or (complicated) the sestet, the sonnet –
None of which beats getting it down plain
Because you're thinking 'bout what you're writing about
And are *on it*.

This is Gaia's gift.

I'm thinking of the diary that you, Gaia, let me read
Which gave me such a lift.
Each day recorded was a joy indeed.

The Fruit of the Word

Apple says 'a' – it was true.
Ah, but the 'a' said 'apple' too.

I'd like to hold again that wee stub of pencil,
Let it make again the mark my mind could never cancel
After the first down-stroke of that slant stem, attached –
Ah! – to the sound of it
In the shape of the fat globe of the round of it,
The first fruit-of-the-word,
The apple.
How it matched
The sound, was the shape
Of that sound, the 'a'
To the apple, the apple to the 'a',
The apple to the 'A'.

Boys and girls: what does the apple say?

Makar Songs, Occasional and Performance Pieces Mainly

Poets Need Not

Poets need not be garlanded;
the poet's head
should be innocent of the leaves of the sweet bay tree,
twisted. All honour goes to poetry.

And poets need no laurels. Why be lauded
for the love of trying to nail the disembodied
image with that one plain word to make it palpable,
for listening in to silence for the rhythm capable
of carrying the thought that's not thought yet?
The pursuit's its own reward. So you have to let
the poem come to voice by footering
late in the dark at home, by muttering
syllables of scribbled lines – or what might
be lines, eventually, if you can get it right.

And this, perhaps, in public? The daytime train,
the biro, the back of an envelope, and again
the fun of the wild goose chase
that goes beyond all this fuss.

Inspiration? Bell rings, penny drops,
the light-bulb goes on and tops
the not-good-enough idea that went before?
No, that's not how it goes. You write, you score
it out, you write it in again the same
but somehow with a different stress. This is a game
you very seldom win
and most of your efforts end up in the bin.

There's one hunched and gloomy heron
haunts that nearby stretch of River Kelvin
and it wouldn't if there were no fish.
If it never in all that greyness passing caught a flash,
a gleam of something, made that quick stab.

That's how a poem is after a long nothingness, you grab
at that anything and this is food to you.
It comes through, as leaves do.

All praise to poetry, the way it has
of attaching itself to a familiar phrase
in a new way, insisting it be heard and seen.
Poets need no laurels, surely?
Their poems, when they can make them happen – even rarely –
crown them with green.

Connecting Cultures

for Commonwealth Day in Westminster Abbey, 2012

I am talking in our lingua franca.
Tell me, do you drive on the left or right?
Is your football team the *Botswana Zebras*
Or *Indomitable Lions of Cameroon?*
Can you take me to *Junkanoo*
And is there a mangrove forest?
Is it true that a lightweight business suit
Is the appropriate city garb and shaking hands
The usual form of greeting?
Are there frigate birds? Diamonds? Uranium?
What is the climate? Is there a typical hurricane season
Or a *wind of change*?
How many miles of coastline in your country?
Is the currency the Kenyan shilling or the
Brunei dollar – or is it also the word for *rain* or *a blessing*?
Do you speak the lingua franca?

Communication can mean *correspondence*,
Or *a connecting passage or channel*, can mean
A means of imparting and receiving information such as
Speech, social media, the press and cinema.
Communications can mean *means of transporting,*
especially troops or supplies.

Commonwealth means
A free association of independent member nations bound by
Friendship, loyalty, the desire for
Democracy, equality, freedom and peace.
Remembering how hard fellow feeling is to summon
When Wealth is what we do not have in Common,
May every individual
And all the peoples in each nation
Work and hope and

Strive for true communication –
Only by a shift and sharing is there any chance
For the Welfare of all our people and Good Governance.

Such words can sound like flagged-up slogans, true.
What we merely say says nothing –
All that matters is what we do.

Random

for Robyn Marsack

on the occasion of the re-opening of the Scottish Poetry Library,
28 October 2015

Go take a book down from the shelf and open it.
Listen, this isn't 'book' but box,
box full of sound you lift the lid on opening.

Yes, open any item in this place and you'll release
some specific human noise and voice and
song that doesn't need a tune to all-the-truer sing.
Pick one. Pick anything.
Slim volume or expansive, all-inclusive, fat anthology –
neither's a dumb tome of texts to tease mere 'meaning' from.
The song's the thing.

And the beauty is, it does away with time and makes it meaningless.
When – this is random, but, say, you flick a page,
here's . . . oh, Ben Jonson
and one man's singular, centuries-old, grief *On my First Son* –
here doth lie, said he,
his best piece of poetrie –
so chimes and rhymes with that here-and-now sorrow of your very
    own
that, hurt by his and stung to tears,
you're somehow almost comforted
because he had the guts to tell it terrible and true.

Love and the other stuff? Well, poets do this too.
Listen, this library-silence thrums
with lyric, epic, L=A=N=G=U=A=G=E, Lallans,
loud hip-hop or rap, maybe the Metaphysicals,
the Silver, Black Mountain, the Beats
and all the big-stuff always – Shakespeare's sonnets,

oor ain bard Burns (*chiefly in the Scots dialect*), Gaelic's *òran mór*.
Here's the murmur of the Modernists,
the auld breath-and-beat of the balladeer –
oh, and – a word in your ear –
they've got a lot of her, thank God, so – *hypocrite lecteur*,
ton semblable, ta soeur et ton frère –
dae mind *Anon*.
She's aye been baith *the real McCoy*
and your perfect contemporary.
All that. And yet it's not cacophony.

Go in. Pick up a book. Enjoy.

Open

on the occasion of the opening of the fourth session of the Scottish Parliament, 2011

'*Open the doors*' wrote the Poet Morgan
eight years ago
on the occasion of the opening of this building,
singing out about 'our dearest deepest wish' –
that the work of this, Our Scottish Parliament, begin
and the 'light of the mind' shine out
as the light of that new day shone in.

Now 'Justice' is a fine and bonny word
to engrave upon a mace
as are: 'Integrity', 'Compassion' and 'Wisdom' –
grand Concepts, qualities to grace
every last thinking person of our Parliament –
but above all: Open-ness.

How else to turn an abstract noun, a name,
into a concrete verb – a *doing word*?
Open your ears, listen, let the people petition and be heard.
Justice, Wisdom, Compassion, Integrity?
Open your eyes – and *see*.

Integrity, Compassion, Justice, Wisdom?
Wisdom, Integrity, Justice, Compassion?
Open your hearts – and hope.
Open your minds – to change.
Open the future – because it's not yet written –
it's as Open as that it's comin' yet is true!
But close the gap between what we say and what we do.

Spring 2010, and at His Desk by the Window is Eddie in a Red Shirt

He likes a red shirt, does Eddie – you should've
seen him last year on his 89th birthday when he
came over to Edinburgh to the Poetry Library for
the opening of his Archive in a scarlet-trimmed
mock-Warhol T-shirt embossed with a metallic
gold, silver and red-striped applique of an iconic
Tunnock's Caramel Wafer with, instead of the
brand-name, *Glasgow*.

He's wearing a red shirt in the photograph
on that page from March, 2005
in the *Herald* that turned up the other day during the
long-overdue big redding-out of my study.
I smile.
Article's about his newly-published *Tales*
from Baron Munchausen. Here
Morgan comes out, again.
This time about his folklorist son Mahmoud he
had to 'the enchanting Leila I met in Cairo
during the Second World War'.
From whose whispering lips, apparently, the
pillow-talk was of the *One*
Thousand and One Nights – initiating
him to this long storytelling life of a poet . . .

But, see, I was wanting to talk of that day back in
the Autumn of 2004.
I've come down to see him with the
embargoed email version of his poem
for the opening of the
new Scottish Parliament Building.
From the photographs he's seen, and celebrated,
Eddie loves it.
Petals . . . curves and caverns, nooks and niches . . .
syncopations and surprises.

Leave symmetry to the cemetery.
But he's too shaky on his pins these days
and, next week, I've to read it
out loud and clear for him on the big day.
Terrifying honour! Four minutes of tongue-twisters.
What do the people want of the place? . . .
A nest of fearties is what they do not want.
A symposium of procrastinators is what they do not want.
A phalanx of forelock-tuggers is what they do not want . . .
Well, we'll rehearse it and mibbe I'll get it right.
He's a good director.
'Liz, *not wholly the power, not yet wholly the power, but . . .*
you're not getting enough out of the
not yet . . .'

Try again.
I'm standing in the open door of the bathroom, declaiming.
There's
amazing Eddie, mild at his neat desk
in this nursing home on the Crow Road.
There's
the dialogue between the cancer cell and the
healthy cell, here're Cyrano, Cathures, Saturn,
Glasgow Green, Cinquevalli, Jesus and Gilgamesh.
randy apples and red shirts and starlings
and strawberries.

When the Poem Went to Prison

after a visit to HM Prison Barlinnie

Apprehensive, the poem goes to prison.
Is photographed, has its bag searched, a form to fill
Checks in money, mobile, rheumatism pills,
Has to declare itself and state its reason.
Brute clang of steel door, bars, barbed wire, fear
Of what they did or didn't do – and that's none
Of the poem's business. Time that must be *done*,
Not lived, *tholed*, scratched off on walls. A love poem? Here?

We could just stey in oor cells, mind, this is oor choice.
Among the din of D Hall, eight men in jail uniform able
To sit down and face the poem, the whole poem,
                    and nothing-but-the-poem around this table.
Gey tremulous to start, it soon will find its voice
And in all innocence, all ears, these men will bless
This grateful love poem with their open-ness.

Listen

Written for the Children's Panel, to encourage new voluntary members, 2012.

Trouble is not my middle name.
It is not what I am.
I was not born for this.
Trouble is not a place
though I am in it deeper than the deepest wood
and I'd get out of it (who wouldn't?) if I could.

Hope is what I do not have in hell –
not without good help, now. Could you
listen, listen hard and well
to what I cannot say except by what I do?

And when you say I do it for badness
this much is true:
I do it for badness done to me before
any badness that I do to you.

Hard to unfankle this.
But you can help me.
Maybe.
Loosen
all these knots and really listen.
I cannot plainly tell you this, but, if you care,
then – beyond all harm and hurt –
real hope is there.

The Silk Road

for Jane as she leaves for her new job in Singapore, 2006

The Silk Road
was the trademark on the motto in the fortune-cookie
I got on China Day when we all
came round the corner from the Art School and
every one of us was
gluttonous on five-spice chicken
in the sunshine
in the Garnethill Garden for the Elderly
and it read:

He who dies with the most toys is nonetheless dead.

Jane, we've never needed fortune-cookie philosophy
to tell us this.
The getting and spending's
never been the thing for either of us and now
we *women of a certain age* know one thing
for certain sure is that there are
no certainties
except
one day (and may
it be many brand new nows from now)
one day, as your father said to you,
our old bones will make very good soup.

So be it. *The intrinsic optimism of curiosity*
this was, someone said,
the key quality of a poet friend of mine.
You own that too.
One thing I know:
for a School of the Creative Arts, anywhere, anywhere,
than you there could be none better.

Already I see you journeying, yes
in the silks of your deconstructed tartan jacket,
in your jet-black beads of felt,
yes felt!, and silver –
(for one thing we women of a certain age have learned
is that things are very seldom made of what they seem . . .)

And the currents of air beneath the wings
are silk banners flying
yes, are the silks of the sky
the clouds beneath you are buoyant as all the
love and the luck that speeds you
from all here who will miss you.

This is China Day and they are
teaching us new ceremonies – so yes
I'll write that wish-label, take it from the pile in the little pavilion
of the Garden for the Elderly
and I'll fling it high,
high in some Scottish tree on this the day of
your festival,
your farewell picnic, and all it'll say

is, 'fly, Jane, fly'.

In Praise of Monsieur Sax

on his 200th Birthday, 6 November 2014

Monsieur Sax, Monsieur Sax, the great Adolphe
Who invented the howl of the urban wolf.
He made the saxotromba, the saxtuba, the saxhorn
Then finally came up with that magical instrument that pure
Caught on!
Yeah, he tinkered with all that brassy trash and then – *tout 'suite* –
Struck gold with the Daddy of them all who could sure
Toot sweet.

Though – as the cliché says –
He came from that place
Famous for nobody but Jacques Brel, the bloke that thought up
    Tintin, and René Magritte –
Adolphe Sax, it was you
It was you,
It was you
Made that thing
That makes that sound
That snarls from midnight Manhattan windows or curls
Like the steam from the grilles in the street,
The sound that howls its blue, blue loneliness then
Coos real low, cool and sweet.

All praise to Monsieur Sax, the blessed Adolphe
Who invented the authentic howl
Of the urban wolf.

Grace

Written for the Royal Incorporation of Architects in Scotland on the occasion of the Annual Fellows Dinner, 2012.

Once in Moab
before *the land of milk and honey*
it was written in Deuteronomy
that before breaking bread together, friends, we should
take pause, and then say grace.
Which was to say we were to bless
what blessed us with everything that was good.
God – or the
land of the wheat and the barley, the
source of all our food,
the land of the vine and the fig and the pomegranate,
the land of the oil-olive and the syrup-date.

This is Scotland, this
our one small country in this great wide world, which is
our one, wondrous, spinning, dear green place.
What shall we build of it, together
in this our one small time and space?

We are far from Deuteronomy,
far from long forgotten
Moab, far from any *land of milk and honey* –
we are where *nothing is written*

Yet tonight
together
for good food and even better fellowship,
whether we have a God or not
our gratitude cannot be denied.

And we shall eat, and we shall be satisfied.

Lines for the Centenary of the Scotch Whisky Association

Freedom an whisky gang thegither – Robert Burns

I

When we sit wined and finely dined,
Dressed up in oor best, braw and fancy,
Oh, it's a far cry tonight, in this company bright,
From the rude and hoorin' howff o Poosie Nancy.
Friends, we hae a history:
Rough stuff. 'Rascally Kilbagie'
Mair fiery by faur than 'lost Ferintosh' and fit,
fit for but 'the most rascally part',
fit for but the bard's Jolly Beggars,
fit only for 'rectifying' into Hollands gin
– in the back lanes of London,
Mother's Ruin.

Sing, drunk for a penny,
Blin fou for tuppence, quaff
An ye shall hae straw for free
When you maun sleep it aff.

II

Two hundred and fifty years . . .
How many thousand bottlings
to the honeyed finish,
aromas of lavender, sherry-cask or gorse;
essences and esters of salt, pine, nutmeg, smoke;
tinctures of topaz, amber, mahogany,
palest straw, purest gold, liquid?
Liquors, elixirs, infused with – is that a
hint of *anise*, even liquorice?

Toddies tea-coloured, smooth and soothing –
can you taste tobacco, heather-nectar, rain or moorland,
smell the sea?
How many thousand bottlings, angel's shares,
new market leaders in the field,
till today's best blends and the triple-distilled?

III

Ask MacDiarmid, ask Ettrick Hogg –
Wha took his whisky 'by the joug' –
Ask Rab himsel, an he will tell you whether –
Language made essence, thought distilled –
Inspiration's whit a dram might yield?
If poetry an whisky gang thegither?
Consider. Answer. Aye, right well thegither.
Though – taken by the jug-fu – either yin's reduced to blether.

IV

And *friendship* an whisky surely gang thegither?
It's the *aqua vitae* we imbibe wi yin another.
A hip-flask in the cauld, uncorked, a shared swig,
A deal sealed wi a word and a dram,
Och, see us a splash of water from thon china jug,
Gie us drappie in my coffee mug,
There's aye a drouth for true companionship, until at last
The luggit cup o the quaich is passed.
Sweetness sipped from a chinked glass, cheers!
Savour friendship.
Its flavour will mature for years.

V

And – if freedom an whisky gang thegither –
How do you like your freedom? Swallowed neat?
Distillations of history, language, weather
In an usqueba o barley, burn water, peat.

From a Mouse

The present author being, from her mother's milk, a lover of the poetic effusions of Mr Robert Burns and all creatures therein (whether mouse, louse, yowe, dug or grey mare Meg) was nonetheless appalled to find, in her slattern's kitchen, sitting up washing its face in her wok, the following phenomenon.

It's me. The eponymous *Moose*
The *To a Mouse* that, were I in your hoose,
A bit o dust ablow the bed, thon dodd o' oose
That, quick, turns tail,
Is – eek! – a *living creature* on the loose,
Wad gar you wail.

Aye, I've heard you fairly scraich, you seem
Gey phobic 'boot Mice in Real Life yet dream
Aboot Man-Mouse Amity? Ye'll rhyme a ream!
Yet, wi skirt wrapt roon,
I've seen ye staun up oan a chair an scream
Like Daphne Broon.

But I'm *adored* – on paper! – ever since
First ye got me at the schule, at yince
Enchantit – wha'd aye thocht poetry was mince
Till ye met Rabbie,
My poor, earth-born companion, an the prince
O *Standard Habbie*.

For yon is what they cry the form *he* wrote in
An' *you* recite. Gey easy, as you ken, to quote in
Because it *sticks.* I will allow it's *stoatin*,
This nifty stanza
He could go to sicc lengths wi, say sicc a lot in –
Largs to Lochranza,

Plockton to Peebles, Dumfries to Dundee,
If a wean kens ony poem aff by hert, it's *me!*
Will greet ower ma plough-torn nest, no see
The bit o' a gap
Atween the fause Warld o' Poetry
An baited trap.

Get Rentokil! Get real! Wha you love
'S the ploughman in the poem, keen to prove
– Saut tears, sigh, sympathy – he's sensitive.
Wee sermon:
Mice, men, schemes agley, Himsel' above
cryin me vermin.

Ploughman? That will be right! *Heaven-taught?*
He drank deep o The Bard, and Gray, and Pope – the lot.
I, faur frae the spontaneous outburst you thought,
Am an artifact.
For Man's Dominion he was truly sorry? Not!
'Twas all an act.

Burns, baith man and poet, liked to dominate.
His reputation wi the lassies wasna great.
They still dinna ken whether they love to hate,
Or hate to love.
He was *an awfy man!* He left them tae their fate,
Push came to shove.

Couldnae keep it in his breeks? Hell's bells, damnation,
I wad be the vera last to gie a peroration
On the daft obsession o this prurient Nation,
His amatory antics.
He was – beating them tae it by a generation –
First o th' Romantics.

Arguably, I am a poem wha, prescient, did presage
Your Twenty-First-Century Global Distress Age.
I'm a female *Moose* though, he didna gie a sausage
For ma sparklin' een!
As for Mother Nature? Whether yez get the message
Remains to be seen.

The Theatre Maker's Credo

for David McVicar, Ralph Riach, Siobhan Redmond, Ann Scott Jones and D.C. Jackson, who are all quoted here

Tell the story
Make it make sense –
Whether you've got a budget of three hundred grand
Or fifty pence
Just tell the story –
In the present tense.

Tell it in prose
Tell it in rhyme
Tell it in words of one syllable
Tell it in mime
Give it the old softshoe
With the once-upon-a-time . . .

Tell it with a soaring operatic aria
Or a wee folk song
Tell it with a pure heart and an open mind
And you won't go far wrong.

Tell it to the World and his Wife –
And their illiterate friend
Who doesn't even know Hamlet
Dies in the end!

Tell it complete with undeleted expletives
Tell it short and sweet
Show it so I'll know it
With a silence, a look, or a beat.
Tell it in extravagant verbal flights of fancy –
Oh *audibly* – gie us a chance! –
Even (over my dead body)
Tell it in dance –

But just tell the story:
Not necessarily loud, but clear.
Don't show me where we're going,
Take me there
By telling me the story –
Let me in.
Are we sitting comfortably?
Then let us begin . . .

Doesn't have to be a new story –
The old ones are, whiles, the best.
Just: is it a good story?
That's the acid test.

What are we human-beings like, eh?
What *have* we got in us?
There's the best of the worst and the worst of the best –
So, *Gather round, picanninies* . . .

Tell it like it is, but!
Don't forget
The isle being full of many noises, plenty brand-new voices
Ain't never been heard from yet!

Spare us the protagonist's monologue
Just show what he or she *does*
And, as old Shakespeare himself says, we'll see
What Hecuba is to us . . .

If you're *determined* to be tragic,
Well . . . gie's the odd laugh, please,
Even if you're up to your oxters in blood –
(Think Euripides).

On the other hand Molière
Was right on the money
With his cast of gloomy obsessives
Who were just so fucking funny.

So take a long look at life, tell the truth,
Play it as it lays –
Oh, plus K.I.S.S. (Keep it Simple, Stupid)
As the Man Mamet says.

Part one of the Process:
Go back to square one
And just tell the story all over again.
Don't forget to have fun,

Let's not get arty, nor earnest
(God, earnest is the worst).
Fuck them if they can't take a joke –
But don't tell the punchline first.

Yeah, tell it in the right order
And you'll really put us through it.
Through hoops, loops, one fell swoops
And Ohmigod! – I knew it . . . !

To hell with telling folk what they should think –
That's just not polite.
Don't try and change people's minds –
Mibbe just try change their night?

For the message is: There is No Message –
Heaven forbid! –
Let the audience *think on* 'bout what happened,
But be damn sure what did!

Though it *is* Show Business Not Tell Business
Nevertheless – have I said this before, eh? –
The business of the whole show
Is to Just Tell the Story.

And though Non-narrative Theatre
Seems to be all the rage –
With the funders – if not the punters –
Let us put on the stage

The one-and-only, ever-loving, rootin'-tootin' Story
Which will out, in the end.
Long live the story
Although it depend –

Whether it's a Living Nightmare
Or a Midsummer Night's Dream –
Yup, depends on each and every member
Of the Creative Team

Not fucking-up the story
(However hard to stage)
And them all telling the Same Story,
Being on the Same Page

Telling it with style and pace
(One to ninety, back to zero).
Do 'get right inside your character' –
Monster, everyman or hero –

But it's not *your* story,
No, it's not about you,
It's not about the Bad Divorce
The leading actor's going through

It's about the *people in the play*
And what happens next.
Just tell the blooming story,
Stick to the text.

In Number One Dressing Room

in celebration of the 2015 re-opening of Glasgow's Theatre Royal

Backstage
in Number One dressing room
on this, the last night of the run,
before *Beginners* and after her *Five-minute Call*
just time for one last time
to centre herself, apply one last scoosh
of that antique cologne she wears to
get in character with just this character,
bin the dregs of it, kiss
her lucky rabbit's-foot mascot that
got her grandad through the war, drop it
in the maw of her packed carpet bag.
She's counted the champagne corks
before chucking them,
unpeeled from their blu-tack all the good-luck cards,
stacked them to save and take on top of those
drawings from her children that
sent
their *lots and lots of love Mummy, Mummy!* but
gave her guilt.

The over-the-top flamboyant flowers
her agent sent are drooped and dying,
ditto the bonny bouquets from friends,
even the single rose from her secret lover.
She smears the lipsticked messages and kisses
on the merciless mirror, risks
a final check in it, bares her teeth.
God, but she's glad of that nap under her wrap
before the half –
one last night to get every last thing right!

There's a plane ticket in her handbag.
Beginners, and out she goes along breezeblock corridors
to the wings, the wings

which give her flight.

Nick Dowp, Feeling Miscast in a Very English Production, Rehearses Bottom's Dream.

Tie up my lover's tongue? Yon's censorship!
Hae anither English apricock and button your lip.
Neither dewberry nor honey bag from humble bee'll keep
Me silent, I hate it!
Fish oot o watter in this green wid, I hope
To funn mysel translatit.

Proud Titania – yon's who yon posh quine is –
She hus a faur, faur better pert than mine is!
Her 'R.P.' Shakespeare-spiel, oh as befits a lady fine, is
In couplet verse.
Whauras I get *mere prose* o which the bottom line is
That I'm an erse!

Shakespeare's, (excuse me for being cynical)
Attitude to Scotch verse is that it's kinna like McGonagall's
And only guid enough for thae Rude-Mechanicals
An Loss-the-Plots
To tumpty-tum their numpty lyricals
In accents Scots

Ach, but here goes! In ma ain wurds!
I have had a maist rare and unco and byornar Vision. I have hud a dream – telling ye, I'm daunerin aroon in a dwamm like a hauf shut knife tryin to shake mysel free o it, but och, it's beyond Man's kennin to say whitlike a dream it wis.
I'm dumfounert, fair dumfounert.
I'm naethin but a cuddy if I ettle to expound upon it at ony length.
See, whit I thocht . . . naw, naw I'm saying nuthin! But, aye! Naw, aye, I thocht I *wis* . . . and I thocht I *hud* . . . and a' the lang nicht lang . . . but you'll get hee-haw oot o me on sicc maitters, Nick Dowp is ower much o a gentleman . . .
Man's een havena heard, man's lugs havena seen, his fummlin, fouterin hauns havena the gumption to taste, nor his tongue to

mak heid nor tail o – naw, nor yet his hammerin hert
to let dab aboot! – whitlike ma dream wis.
I'll mibbe get somebody to write it doon for me to elocute?
In *the Doric*, do they no cry it? Them that canna thole *keelie-talk*, nor
kailyerd, nor the *deservedly much despisit and debasit accents o the urban poor?* Sicc snobs! I say: love-o-goad almighty, could somebody no mibbe dae somethin hauf-wey guid in the Glesca-patois to gie us a laugh and let me an the Mechanicals sook in with the Duke an his Leddy at the finish-up o oor play?

For oor cast has a wheen o erses to kiss
Us workin-joes, we hae to hae a hit, we canny miss!
And still we areny really oot the wids wi this
Heedrum-hodrum humdrum –
For thon Shakespeare-felly thocht it funny to take the piss
Oot o am-dram!

So his jiner, tylor, wabster are no very smart
But guid-herted cheils gey willin to learn their part –
Only when it gets richt spooky dae they get feart,
Rin awa in alarm.
An I dream! Mindin it will aye wind aroon my heart
Like a hairy worm!

Epistle to David

for David MacLennan (1948–2014), a fellow theatre-maker

The heart aye's the part aye – Robert Burns: Epistle to Davie,
A Brother Poet

Dear David, I scribble this because today
We did the read-through of your 300th play –
We open in two short weeks (eek!) on Monday 20th May –
Imagine! Three hundred plays which did not exist before
They *premiered at one p.m.* at Òran Mór.

OK, flashback. Best part of a decade ago,
So the story goes and as far as I know,
Once upon a time in the West – Byres Road t'be exact –
You, David McL, bumped into one Colin Beattie, who was, matter
of fact,
Up to his oxters in turning a derelict church into a dream he had.
He (you-don't-have-to-be-crazy-etc.-but-it-helps) was mad
To make it much more than a super-pub and mega wedding
destination,
Was dying to show you the story-so-far of his new creation,

So he jams a hard-hat on your heid and . . . in you baith go.
David, you could not believe your eyes (at least you told me so) –
Th'whole place, the space, the colour, the light,
Stained-glass, half-restored splendour, and – at a great height –
Alasdair Gray on his back on scaffolding, a latterday Michelangelo
Painting Sistine-esque intricacies on the ceiling – and, D, what
d'you know,
Colin goes: What would *you* like to do in this venue?
You don't blink, don't even think, just open your mouth and then
you
Come out with your *own* mad idea, and, as a result, you
Are a legend in your own lunchtime – which is not to insult you,

In fact, D, it prompts this fond epistle – I just thought: ach, might as well,
In praise of you, old pal, Producer Extraordinaire,
Produce a line or twa o doggerel?

Because, thon fateful day, this was your reply:
I've got a good idea. Hey Colin, why
Don't we do Lunchtime Theatre here?
Say it's: *A Play, A Pie, and A Pint?* Let's try . . .
They pay us tenner, they get a play, they get a pint, they get a pie.
C'mon, Colin, say aye!

And the rest (as they say) is history.
From that first season – September 2004, the first of twelve plays
To the annual thirty-eight productions and forty-two weeks of nowadays.

Whit Taggart was it you were in?
Actors used to get asked this all the time, before.
Now it's: *Haw, when did you last dae an Òran Mór?*

Could be a monologue, a musical, a comedy, a tragedy, a panto, a rom-com
Just check it out on double-u, double-u, double-u dot playpiepint dot com.
All hail PPP – a veritable and a venerable fixture
With a welcome-to-all-comers
Open-to-all-ideas repertoire that's a total mixture.

Say you're a brand new writer –
Or one new at least to writing plays –
Òran Mór's audience'll fairly teach you how to play it as it lays.
It is hard to get a start, but, David, you're out to change that.
As for us old hands – you're aye careful to arrange that
We don't feel left behind either, don't feel . . . left out,
That we drop our jaded attitudes, are . . . still in with a shout?
David I confess today it made me very proud

To hear my wee three-hander – your 300th play –
If not yet up on its feet, at least *out loud.*

But, though the play's the thing,
You do like to tell it like it is, D
(I'm remembering *Dear Glasgow*, those *Letters From the Arab Spring*)
Oh, it's a big wide world and –
We want to tell you a story
We want to make it make sense
We know what the gig is –
To tell the story in the present tense.
Yes, we'll just tell the story;
Not necessarily *loud*, but clear.
Won't show the audience where we're going,
Just take them there
By telling them the story, David,
Letting them in,
We'll go, *Are we sitting comfortably?*
Then let us begin . . .

Portrait of a Gentleman at Sixty

for Ralph Riach

In fair Rose Terrace there lives a man
Of grace, of style, *d'un certain* age and pure élan.
He is always elegant, it matters not a toss
Whether 'tis kilt, socks and sandshoes, or Hugo Boss . . .
He likes a good joke wi sweerin, he is, let's say no prude,
But it must be rhythmical, inventive, funny and no jist crude.

And he knows the Rare Occasion when 'twill not quite do
To tell the tale of the Broon Coo and the White Coo.
When fans accost him, how graciously he bends to answer
Their *who urr you again? Settle a bet! Were you in* Chancer?
Naw! It's thingwy ooty whidjie, whit is it you're on?
Were you the baddie in – Naw! It's TV John!

May his every *Taggart* get re-repeated!
May his every *Guardian Crossword* get completed!
May Redmond phone him up and go *Hey, tell us*
What is fifteen down? . . . And then get pure jealous!

May he get his country cottage, the sort eh?
Where he may freely play his piano, forte!
May he (and all the other Hamish MacBeth individuals)
Get yet another series at double fees plus residuals.

He is never O.T.T. We may always expect
Minimum effort, maximum effect.
His timing's nice, he is often praised
As master of the demi-beat, the eyebrow not quite raised.
We appreciate his talent, but each appreciator
Knows his talent for friendship is even greater.
No better pal than he, ach,
Many Happy Returns to you, Ralph Riach.

Address to a Septuagenarian Gentleman at Home

for Ralph Riach

Gardener's Cottage. Des Res is not the word!
Out of the poky wee sow's ear that was Bon Accord
You made such a silken purse. Oh, the trouble
You took to coax this floribundant garden from the rubble
A green-fingered glory; to furnish this home-from-home
With a welcome warm enough to make all comers come
From A' the Airts and Pairts for R&R
For music, food and friendship, for Just You to be the way you are
Our dear Ralph, a genial generous host to either pop in on
Else stay (and stay) till any other bugger'd say, *Begone!*
Och, gie any of us an inch and we'll take a mile!
But, Christ, you even nag our arses off with style.

Seventy summers. Three score and ten
Could be considered a good age! In lesser men
Well, fuck it, let's face it, *tempus fugit*
And we're all knocking on a bit – but you don't look it.
To say 'You wear it well' is to state the obvious
And you're the most likely of all of us
To – thirty years hence – have Prince William
(Once he's the King) send you That Telegram.

Meanwhile, may you have sunshine in the garden a.m. till p.m.,
Many, many Methven Arms lunches, new piano pieces, *carpe diem*!
Oh and *carpe per diems* as well,
For I wish you more parts in films than tongue can tell,
That many lucrative wee tellies
As to make all your many thespian friends pure jealous.

May there be acres of that bonny needlepoint cross-stitchin'
Tapestry to blossom at your fingertips in Mrs Jolly's Kitchen.
May your every cross word be in the *Guardian*

May you be daily forced to phone a friend and say, 'A hard yin,
Right enough, it was today, but me, I got it done –
Even that hoor-o-a-clue eight down! – by early afternoon.
See, I'm aye on Araucaria's wavelength, that wee twist
I enjoy much more than Bunthorne or Enigmatist!'

May we watch *Bullets Over Broadway* 'til we know it off by heart.
All the lines, not just Chazz Palminteri's part.
May we bring many a new year together, would be good, eh?
And you could show us Elaine Stritch, Ethel M. and Judy.
Long may we have to swither 'ere we can decide
Whether to have smoked salmon in our scrambled eggs or on the
  side.

Dearest Ralph, I wish you all you wish yourself, but selfishly,
I wish you many hours to spend with *me*!

For Myra McFadden on her Sixtieth Birthday

Surely some mistake! Better get it fixed eh?
A little bird told me
That Myra's sixty!
Sixty?
Sixty?
Surely no!
Surely no!
Jeepers, creepers
who's that girl in them tartan brothel creepers?
Aye it's Myra,
Myra
oor Myra.

You can keep your Little Eva,
you can keep your Brenda Lee,
though her voice penetrates like theirs do
– and though she's *wee* –
you can keep your Little Eva
you can keep your Brenda Lee
'cos Myra, she's the girl for me.
Myra, she sing rock 'n' roll
she sing sweet, she sing low
she sing loco
she sing local
she sing like a lintie in a leafy tree
Myra she's the zinging singing girl for me.

If I was Ian Dury, if I could sing,
(although, God only knows,
my singing scores
even less than well-below-zero)
but I say, if I could
I surely would
do for Myra what sweet Dury did
for Gene Vincent, his hero.

Myra's friends – and, oh my God,
oor Myra's friends are myriad –
wanted those most of us who can't be there at your party
to record a wee memory of some bit of fun we've had
(and digitally?
Ohmigod, give-me-a-break I'm a Luddite, that willnae be me
but I'm supposed to . . . document this memory?)
OK, voice memo and
been wracking my brains for the right anecdote
and I can't – well I've got *plenty* – but not one
she'd want me to *quote* . . .

She's a wonderful friend to be on-the-same-page with
she's a very dangerous woman to be on the same stage with
(ask Siobhan,
ask Siobhan,
ask anyone!)
Give her one line, give her . . . a look
and no one else will get a look-in, hey,
don't even give her the song she so deserves
just give her one note
and who's the star of the show?
Myra! Myra always gets everybody's vote.
She's the one that everybody remembers
in musicals, comedies and dramas
because she's the dog's bollocks and the cat's pyjamas.

You all will have got the picture:
I simply think she's great
but *Sixty?* (well, suppose she must be since I am sixty-eight . . .)
and, because for half her life I've always known what like she is
you can bet your ass
I'm dying to see what that girl's gonna do
with her freedom pass

Myra – what's she like, eh?
Myra, Myra –
tho we all love her to bits – she's *oor Myra, your Myra, abody's Myra* –

and tho – like every other bugger – I am her greatest admirer
I just canny put it intae words, she's
just Myra!
Myra, ach, impossible to describe her.
You just have to get in her company and
positively imbibe her!

What's she like?
What's she like, eh?
Mama mia, just ask Zanna
– they're each other's love, life, pride and joy –
so just ask Zanna
whether Ms Myra McFadden ain't the real McCoy?

Song for a Dirty Diva

Why are my friends all friends of Dorothy?
Now, I'm cool and glib about gay lib
But suddenly it's got to me
That all of my friends are friends of Dorothy.

Now, I get on great in gay bars and the boys adore me –
We even fancy the same film stars and the crack is frank and free.
They'll do my clothes, my hair, my decor
But they won't do me.

Yet I can go some from here to kingdom come.
Hey, man, you must be barmy
If you think you could exhaust me, yeah, you and
Whose army?
I could ball a rugby team and cream them all to orgasm.
Take a caveman, and his club, to fill ma yawnin chasm.

All those guys who're really nice, but not interested,
All those nancies who don't fancy the tried and tested,
Who turn the other cheek and spurn
What can't be bested,
Oh they huff and they puff and they get real vexed
About my mainstream addiction to
Hetero-sex.

My thoroughly modern girlfriends all say to me
You aint tried it don't knock it you should suck it and see.
I say thanks a lot but no thanks
It's not for me.

I want a real man with a rock-hard dose of the horn
Who these days is as rare as
A unicorn.
Oh I wish he'd pure skewer ma penetralia
And spatter ma sheets with a map of Australia

But 'cause all my pals who are gals
Are strictly Sapphic
They seem to deem it disgustin' and pornographic.
But my sex life's at a standstill –
There is no through traffic
So – at the risk of sounding politically incorrect –
I need a crash-course collision
With something erect.

Yet all of my friends are friends of Dorothy,
Yeah, friends of Dorothy.
Now, I'm cool and glib about gay lib
But suddenly it's got to me
That all of my friends are friends of Dorothy.
And why oh why do they get that vexed
About my mainstream addiction to
Hetero-sex?

Another, Later, Song for that Same Dirty Diva

'Just visiting, honey? Dream on . . .
This, ma darlin', is the ladies' john
Of the Seniors Association of Greater Edmonton
And Ah'm here to tell you, girl, one fine day
You're going to find yourself permanently here in the Sunshine Café
Fitting in perfectly among us old-timers
With the arther-itis and the arteriosclerosis and the
Alz-heimers.
– Which is *not* my problem, baby –
No, cruel thing is I can *remember* way back when still
Ah'd some ooze in ma cooze
And he'd a leettle lead in his pencil.
OK, these days it's not the same
But give it a little elbow grease and I'm still game.
Though when you are more
Than three-score-
And-ten
It's very fucking unlikely to be raining men.
Soon you, too, will be grubbing round for the *last* of the
Last-of-the-red-hot-lovers
'Mong the 'lasticated leisure-suits and the
Comb overs . . .

Ah, it was a very good year – yeah, back in
Nineteen-fifty sumthin' when ma sex life was jus' begun
And the fact you *shouldn't* was . . . jus' part of the fun.
(Oh boy, the joy
Of being underage, oversexed and in the back
Of someone's daddy's Cadillac . . .)
Soon the swinging sixties
And ooh baby I swung,
Got all the action that was going –
And plenty – in ma twenties when I was young . . .
The permissive society? Remember?
A great club. I was happy to be a member.

Fantastic! Fuck-all forbidden
'N everybody perked up at the prospect
Of bein'
Bed-ridden.
Yes, in sixty-nine it was a very good year . . . damn fine
For moon-landings and . . . sixty-nine.
And in the seventies did I slow up a tad?
Not a whit, not a bit of it. Are you mad?
For there was *always* sex-and-drugs and having a laugh –
When 'a selfie' was certainly not a
Photograph.

Ah, once there was
Powder in the powder room –
You could get it on, no bother
And every which way,
When two-in-a-cubicle used to mean something other
Than what it means today.
Remember, before?
When *two* paira shoes, under one locked door
Signalled sex, illicit and acrobatic?
Now it's likely to be 'a carer' and 'a client', geriatric.

Once there were
Pills, poppers,
Downers, uppers,
All on offer – and no lack o'
More than a whiff of more than a spliff of that wacky tobacco.
Now ma handbag still harbours drugs of every description
But these days, darlin',
They are all prescription.'

And she snapped her lipstick back in her purse,
Gave me a wink that said: 'Could be worse'.
Yes, she said all this with a single look.
It was eloquent (oh, I could read her like a book).
It said,
'Forget the nips and tucks, they are not the answers.'

And off she hobbled to join her team
Of geriatric line-dancers.

Yes, off she went leaving me alone
Before the mirror in the ladies' john.
It felt a little flat without her . . .
She left a kinda . . . absence in her wake.
I sighed and looked around me and then, fuck-sake,
Saw something I'd never seen the like of, never since
They started dishing out the complimentary condoms in the
Eighties, remember? Yes. Like . . . after dinner mints?

Well, what can I say?
That day
In the female comfort-station of the Sunshine Café,
There, then, in the ladies' john
Of the Seniors Association of Greater Edmonton,
Bold as brass, gratis and for free,
Openly out there on the counter between the soap dispenser and the
Potpouri
Right before my very eyes
Lo and behold, very much to my surprise –
Free incontinence supplies!

In Praise of Old Vinyl

In the beginning was the chord
The perfect combo of the melody and the word
Played at thirty-three and a third

Four in the morning, crapped out, yawning
Still crazy after all these years.

    Old vinyl . . . old vinyl
    Nostalgia's everything it used to be
    When you're half-pissed and playing that old LP

You make me feel . . . You make me feel . . . You make me feel –
It's not-so-easy listening without protection
When you open Pandora's Record Collection –
May you never lay your head down
Without a hand to hold
Lord knows when the cold wind blows it'll turn your head around
Little things I should have said and done
I just never took the time
But I always thought I'd see you a –
No more I love yous
Language is –
Hey that's no way to say
Go way from my window
Leave at your own chosen speed
I'm not the one you want babe
I'm not the one you need
I keep singing them sad, sad songs, y'all
Sad songs is all I know.

Talking 'bout the box you've never even opened since your last flit
Full of all you could rescue from that Bad Split –
The albums, seminal and antique,
You saved up pocket-money for, week after week –
The ones that took your teenage soul apart,

The ones that broke your thirty-something heart,
The ones you stole from old lovers,
With muesli in the grooves, coffee-stains on the covers
And printed lyrics that that were pure
Lonely bedsitter literature –
I learned the truth at seventeen . . .

Oh Dusty and Joni and Nico and Emmylou,
Dylan, Van-the-Man and Rhymin' Simon too . . .
Songs to flood you with all that came to pass
Between 'Piece of My Heart' and 'Heart of Glass'
Once had a love and it was a gas . . .

    Old vinyl . . . old vinyl
    Nostalgia's everything it used to be
    When you're half-pissed and playing that old LP

Annie and K.D. and Eddi and Ella for when you're home alone
Inventing a lover on the . . . Saxophone!
When he's gone and you and those lonesome blues collide
A certain Canyon Lady knows just how you feel inside . . .
The bed's too big, the frying pan's too wide

Furry sings the blues? Well, if anybody can,
Sincerely L. Cohen – you're my man.
And (oh my sweet lord and he's so fine)
Gravel-voiced Tom Waits with his Blue Valentine –
An' Otis 'n Elvis 'n some-kinda-Wonderful Stevie were the men
When you picked yourself up 'n tried to love again –
But . . . Baby I know – the first cut is the deepest . . .

    Old vinyl . . . old vinyl
    Nostalgia's everything it used to be
    When you're half-pissed and playing an old LP . . .

I want to walk in the open wind
I want to talk like lovers do
I want to dive into your ocean
Is it raining with you?

Come on, c'mon, c'mon, don't kid on
You don't remember when
Yesterday was young and it was raining men?
Believe me . . . believe me . . .
Though it's an achey-breaky this-old-heart of yours – it's murder –
Old Stereo's still in working order!
Needle gets in the groove and proves as it plays
That all tomorrow's parties are now yesterday's.
From Sinatra to Suzi Quatro to Suzanne
It takes a lot of pain, it takes a lot of pain
Love hurts, love scars, love wounds and mars,
ooh ooh love hurts . . .

But – oh sex and drugs and rock and roll! –
Buddy Holly, Billie Holiday and Billy Fury,
Janis Joplin, Janis Ian and Ian Dury
Have little in common, as a matter of fact,
Except – one hook, and they fair take you back!
I'm sorry that I made you cry . . .
Apple, Island, Rough Trade, HMV and Stiff
Label me, turntable me, and let me riff!
Do me wrong, do me right, tell me lies but hold me tight . . .
Oh and you'll be back in love again, back at school,
back in the USS – back where your memories will unspool
like that audio-cassette your midnight-caller compiled
With Easy-like-Sunday-Morning and Born-To-Be-Wild

He comes for conversation . . .

> Old vinyl . . . old vinyl
> Nostalgia's everything it used to be
> When you're half-pissed and playing that old LP . . .

May you nev – may you nev – may you nev – may you nev –

Oh hear those nice, bright colours,
Hear the greens of summers,
You'll be wearing rags and feathers from Salvation Army counters,
You'll be Marcie in a coat of flowers –
Mama, please don't take my Parlophone away.

Old vinyl . . . old vinyl . . .

Acknowledgements

Some of these poems have appeared online and in other publications: 'In the Mid-Midwinter'; 'Connecting Cultures'; 'Random'; 'Listen' and 'Lines for the Centenary of the Scotch Whisky Association'; all first appeared on the Scottish Poetry Library website. 'How I'll Decorate My Tree' appeared on the Poetry Society website. 'A Handselling, 2006' was published in *The Sprit of Jura* (Polygon, 2009). 'Glasgow Nonsense Rhyme, Nursery Rhyme, for Molly' appeared in *The Thing that Mattered Most: Scottish Poems for Children*, edited by Julie Johnstone (Black & White, 2006). 'Song for a Dirty Diva' first appeared in *The Colour of Black & White: Poems 1984–2003* (Polygon, 2003). 'Nick Dowp, Feeling Miscast in a Very English Production, Rehearses Bottom's Dream'; 'Some Old Photographs' and 'In Alan Davie's Paintings' were published in *New Poems Chiefly in the Scottish Dialect*, edited by Robert Crawford (Polygon, 2009). 'Persimmons'; 'Wedding Vow'; 'When the Poem Went to Prison' and 'Poets Need Not' all first appeared in *A Choosing: Selected Poems* (Polygon, 2011).